Difficult Ornaments

Difficult Ornaments

Florida and the Poets

ANGE MLINKO

OXFORD
UNIVERSITY PRESS

OXFORD
UNIVERSITY PRESS

Oxford University Press is a department of the University of Oxford.
It furthers the University's objective of excellence in research, scholarship,
and education by publishing worldwide. Oxford is a registered trade mark of
Oxford University Press in the UK and in certain other countries.

Published in the United States of America by Oxford University Press
198 Madison Avenue, New York, NY 10016, United States of America.

© Oxford University Press 2024

All rights reserved. No part of this publication may be reproduced,
stored in a retrieval system, or transmitted, in any form or by any means,
without the prior permission in writing of Oxford University Press,
or as expressly permitted by law, by license or under terms agreed with
the appropriate reprographics rights organization. Inquiries concerning
reproduction outside the scope of the above should be sent to
the Rights Department, Oxford University Press, at the address above.

You must not circulate this work in any other form
and you must impose this same condition on any acquirer

Library of Congress Cataloging-in-Publication Data
Names: Mlinko, Ange, author.
Title: Difficult ornaments : Florida and the poets / Ange Mlinko.
Description: New York : Oxford University Press, 2024.
Identifiers: LCCN 2024012681 | ISBN 9780197776551 (hardback) |
ISBN 9780197776575 (epub)
Subjects: LCSH: American poetry—History and criticism. |
Florida—In literature. | Poetics.
Classification: LCC PS310.F56 M55 2024 |
DDC 811/.0099759—dc23/eng/20240516
LC record available at https://lccn.loc.gov/2024012681

DOI: 10.1093/9780197776582.001.0001

Integrated Books International, United States of America

Laura (Riding) Jackson, "All Nothing, Nothing" from *The Poems of Laura Riding:
A New Edition from the 1938 Collection*. Copyright © 1980. Used by permission
of Persea Books, New York. All rights reserved.

To all the poetry teachers

Contents

Preface ix
1. Biological Ornament, Difficult Ornament 1
2. Wallace Stevens: Green Cocoanut Ice Cream 29
3. Marianne Moore: Piracy and Unicorn Horns 47
4. Elizabeth Bishop: A Queer Antique Musical Instrument Floating in the Sea 68
5. James Merrill: Silver Springs and Manatee Kisses 93
6. Harry Mathews: Cool Gales 109
   Epilogue: Laura Riding Jackson 132

Endnotes 147
Bibliography 153
Acknowledgments 157
Index 159

Preface

This is a book about the works that six twentieth-century American poets created—or, in one case, refused to create—in and about the state of Florida. Those poets who nourished their muse on Florida's landscape, history, and myths in turn helped perpetuate those myths: they keep an idea of Florida alive in the cultural imagination and in the language. They were not regional poets, because they did not live there permanently. But they do contribute to a psychogeography: theirs is a Florida that one can access from anywhere in the world through the pages of their books.

This is not a work of Florida history or sociology, nor have I provided a comprehensive biography of these poets. What I have written is a lyrical meditation on style that ranges chronologically, sometimes reaching back to the Elizabethan age or ancient Greek mythology, to better understand the relationship between persons and places, weather and language, the climate of the planet and the climate of the mind.

It so happens that these poets compose a chain of personal friendship and influence: Marianne Moore was friendly with Wallace Stevens, Elizabeth Bishop was friendly with Moore, and James Merrill was friendly with Bishop and socialized frequently with Harry Mathews when both had houses in Key West. Only Riding, who rose to prominence in the 1920s, gave up poetry around 1941, and moved to Wabasso in 1943 to live an isolated existence, stands apart. And yet there are correspondences to be drawn between her work and Merrill's, for instance.

Each poet takes a different approach to their subject. What binds them, however, is fundamental to poetry: a passion for language and its ability to communicate not just abstractly, mind to mind, but also materially, between bodies—through patterned sounds and stresses, through visual imagery, and through word play. The word *play* is essential here: poetry is nothing if not experimental in its attempts to convey experience and perception. In this way, it is like nature itself, and the nearer to the tropics—nature's own laboratory of invention and experiment—the more fecund it is. For this reason, I propose, entirely playfully, that the ornaments of poetry correspond to the ornaments of nature, which is why the peacock, that most decorated of birds, features so prominently in the work of so many poets. That both biologists and literary critics use the word *ornament* to describe the extras of beauty strikes me as no accident. I hope readers will be convinced of the many secret springs of pleasure that lie in our language, given the maps that these poets provide.

"The greatest poverty is not to live
In a physical world."

—Wallace Stevens

"The alphabet's such a horn
Of plenty. Why cork up its treasure?"

—Harry Mathews

1
Biological Ornament, Difficult Ornament

When Juan Ponce de Leon claimed this peninsula for the king of Spain, he named it "Florida" for two reasons: that day, April 2, 1513, was only six days after Easter—called "Sunday of Flowers" in Spanish—and the land looked to be festooned with flowers.

Don Juan, as he is called in *Names on the Land*, the classic by George R. Stewart, also gave the Dry Tortugas their name. Actually, "Dry" was a later addition, alerting mariners to the lack of fresh water. This macaronic mash-up of two languages is also found in "Key West," from *Cayo hueso*, except instead of translating *hueso*, "bone," whoever named Key West simply transliterated it to denote the farthest island of an archipelago bearing southwest.

Why, Stewart wondered, does English place the accent on the first syllable of Florida, when Spanish places it on the second syllable? "The reason for Flórida is, I think, that it has the same spelling and is so pronounced in Latin....In the sixteenth century many books and maps were printed in Latin, and many more Englishmen were familiar with the language than with Spanish. By this theory the name would always have been pronounced in English as Flórida. I have tried to find the name in verse, to check the accentuation."[1] The flow of languages into American English is like a mighty watershed: Spanish, Latin, French, and Indigenous tongues were just a few that happened to converge in Florida. One expects a watershed to produce environs rich with all kinds of wildlife. Poetry is language that challenges our perceptual boundaries, and the greater the diversity of its resources, the more robust it is.

One poet, Elizabeth Bishop, called Florida "the state with the prettiest name":

> the state that floats in brackish water,
> held together by mangrove roots
> that bear while living oysters in clusters,
> and when dead strew white swamps with skeletons,
> dotted as if bombarded with green hummocks
> like ancient cannon-balls sprouting grass.
>
> ("Florida")

And Wallace Stevens, before her, wrote of "the immense dew of Florida," which "brings forth/The big-finned palm/And green vine angering for life" ("Nomad Exquisite").

In their efforts to faithfully depict the natural abundance of Florida—its sheer vegetal plenitude—poets have reached for images of the Edenic and the Jurassic, the primitive and the mythic. But for a succession of poets in the twentieth century who are linked to each other through stylistic hijinks, starry admiration, and devotion to Modernism, Florida was an exotic detour. None was born here. High culture did not exist here. Florida was an idea: sensually intriguing, but also an abstraction that could be worked out in verse. Their versions of Florida perhaps never existed except in the spell cast by their poems, but the fact that all of them did pass a number of years in a veracious Florida raised up out of a land mass of calcified marine skeletons and flooded with sunshine and hurricanes falls somewhere between coincidence and significance. This book rummages around in that gap.

I, too, came here by circumstance—for gainful employment (in, of all places, Gainesville). And I, too, found it exotic, in comparison to the Northeast, where I was born and raised and lived until the very month I turned forty. Exotic, yet disquieting: not having four seasons, for instance, feels like a perturbation of the earth's axis. There is no showy fall foliage. The citrus trees are lovely, but where are the crocuses and tulips and lilacs? Why can't I grow tarragon? I thought I could have a Mediterranean garden in the Florida climate, easy; instead, I found that there is barely any soil—the grass, which is not real grass but a drought-friendly rhizome called St. Augustine, grows in the sand. Monsoon-level rains wash the sand right out from under it in late summer. The terrain is always shifting. Absent the monsoons, the earth dries out very quickly; all the moisture wicks down into the aquifer. Poised between drought and flood, gardeners actually water their lawns in the rainy season.

The beauty of the place—if you can call it that—creeps up on you: literally, in the case of anoles and iguanas and cockroaches, banana spiders and turtles, Brobdingnagian dragonflies and butterflies, many and various bird species. No tarragon, but the alligator steals into the imagination.

*

Florida wasn't the first state I had in mind when I started considering the relation of geography to poetic style. As a teenager in the Philadelphia suburbs, I foraged through the plentiful used bookstores in an area thick with old liberal arts colleges, and so I cut my teeth on the Modernists, from William Butler Yeats and T. S. Eliot to Sylvia Plath and Robert Lowell. It was the Modernists who dominated the New Critical textbooks, the castoff textbooks that overflowed from the shelves. Was it a coincidence that Stevens, Ezra Pound, Marianne Moore, William Carlos Williams, Gertrude Stein, and Hilda Doolittle (H.D.) either were born there or passed through at formative moments? Philadelphia was a subduction zone for poetic Modernism, the last faint seismic waves of which reached me as far into the future as 1985.

Stevens is indelibly associated with Hartford, Connecticut, where he is buried, but he was born in the aptly named Reading,

Pennsylvania. Moore was born in Kirkwood, Missouri, but was raised in south central Pennsylvania before attending Bryn Mawr and then seeking her fortunes in New York, settling at last in Brooklyn. H.D. was born in Bethlehem, Pennsylvania, descended from the Moravian sect who founded the town, though she migrated to Europe and died in Zurich. Ezra Pound was born in Idaho and died in Venice, Italy, where he is buried, but he was raised in Upper Darby in Delaware County, Pennsylvania; his father worked at the US mint in Philadelphia. Helen Carr, in her group biography *Verse Revolutionaries*, reports that when Pound was freed from the Washington, DC, mental asylum where he was sentenced after his trial for treason, he first went back to his childhood home to hug an old tree in the front yard. Then he packed up and went back to Italy forever.

Pound was H.D.'s first boyfriend. They met at a Halloween party in 1901: She was fifteen, he just sixteen, but already a first-year undergraduate at Penn. He had "Gozzoli bronze-gold" curls and wore a green Tunisian robe, every inch the flamboyant troubadour the world would come to know.[2] She wrote about their relationship in two separate memoirs—*End to Torment* and *HERmione*; it would be forever entwined with the color green, and green with Pennsylvania: "This is the forest of Pennsylvania. The murmuring pines and hemlocks." H.D.'s first kisses were with Pound in the woods. *The Gift*, still another memoir of her childhood, is also intensely preoccupied with the Pennsylvania landscape.

Wallace Stevens was somewhat abashed to admit that life, for most people, was "an affair of people not of places. But for me, life is an affair of places and that is the trouble."[3] When he wasn't writing about Florida or Connecticut, he was remembering Pennsylvania, as in "The Countryman," his late poem about a tributary of the Susquehanna River: "Swatara, Swatara, black river…"

Ostensibly in the temperate zone, southeastern Pennsylvania lies just above the Mason–Dixon line and enjoys the deciduous lushness of the mid-Atlantic, neither as subtropical as the South nor as wintry as New England and upstate New York, where the trees aren't quite as thick trunked and broad canopied. What the landscape might suggest to poets in search of a style are horticultural variety, a sinuous terrain of peaks and valleys, and dark and plentiful sources and tributaries.

It is a fair question to ask what would have become of me if I hadn't been raised in southeastern Pennsylvania, so close to this dense poetic history—if I had been raised, say, in rural Florida instead.

*

In fact, northern Florida can fill me with a nameless dread: the flatness, the heat, the rural malaise. The way a hurricane can lay an electric blanket atop the entire state. The high, high trees, a jungle that it seems I cannot outdrive but must be airlifted from. If the days seem like the brightest in the world, the very sunshine acquiring mass and weight, the nights are the darkest I've ever experienced. The first few times I drove at night, on two-lane county roads between Gainesville and the Palm Coast, were eerie—the walls of foliage black as ink, my headlights sopped up by a wilderness on all sides. At times I worried I would always miss city life up north. I thought of Frank O'Hara's famous quote, "One need never leave the confines of New York to get all the greenery one wishes—I can't even enjoy a blade of grass unless I know there's a subway handy, or a record store or some other sign that people do not totally *regret* life."[4] He came to Florida during World War II to train as a sonarman, noted the massive cockroaches and watered-down whiskey, and wrote, "Except for the sky being so near, the dewy stars and the sea, I loathed Key West. Its only excuse for being there is that Wallace Stevens wrote a poem about it."[5]

It was not so very long ago that this county was all backwoods. To go to Marjorie Kinnan Rawlings's house, built in 1884—a few miles down the road—is to come face to face with settler austerities. Her rustic guest house looks like a child's play log cabin with small rooms and dainty windows. Walls, floors, and ceilings are the same unadorned pinewood. There are hurricane lamps on the tables set with crockery; a shelf along the wall features canned goods with long-gone labels, mason jars, cast iron pans, and kettles. In the bedrooms, there are hooks on the walls instead of closets, wash basins instead of baths; the beds are narrow pallets with homespun rag quilts. Wooden crates substitute for tables, rocking chairs for sofas. Everything looks uncomfortable, durable, handmade. I picture living out here in the swamp with my shotgun and my dogs and horses—a rooster and his hens still have the run of the grounds—and I feel as if a bell jar has just descended on me. This was where she wrote *The Yearling*; I have never been able to finish the whole thing. The atmosphere of hardship and emotional privation is too desolate.

There are simply different kinds of imagination. A man I once met—he had been a cave diver for thirty years—pressed a copy of Michel Tournier's *Friday* into my hands; it was his favorite book, a retelling of *Robinson Crusoe*. I read it with admiration for the resourceful style but a shudder of horror at the premise. The dream of starting over from scratch—of building a world, *my* world, self-sufficient—held no appeal for me, but over the years I started to notice those to whom it did. It was a whole new distinction, like W. H. Auden's division of writers into "Mabels" and "Alices." I now was on the qui vive for Crusoe types—and knew that I was not one of them.

Could the origin of my dread lie in the story of the lost colony of Roanoke Island, in what is now North Carolina—a story whose vague outlines were conveyed to me in an elementary school social studies class and which has haunted me ever since? In 1586, 116 English settlers, under the auspices of Queen Elizabeth I and the direction of Sir Walter Raleigh, settled a fort on Roanoke Island previously built by Raleigh's men. After a desperately long wait for provisions delayed by England's war with Spain, the colonists seemingly vanished with barely a trace. When their appointed governor, John White, returned in 1590 to rescue them, he found a fort swept clean of any sign of human habitation. (White's own granddaughter was among the missing: Virginia Dare, the first English baby born in the New World.) The word *CROATOAN* was carved into a tree, the only clue; but when he set a course for the island of Croatoan, they weren't there either. The mystery was never solved.

The reality of founding a settlement in the wilderness seemed at stark odds with the Crusoe fantasy. If the ravages of an unfamiliar climate and farming conditions posed one danger, hostile natives posed another. But there was no danger worse than one's rival colonists. The lovely beach I take my kids to, an hour and a half drive to the east, is called Matanzas—the Spanish word for slaughter. It was so named because the (Catholic) Spanish massacred the (Protestant) French survivors of a shipwreck in 1565; those Frenchmen had been on their way to attack the Spaniards' fort at St. Augustine, while the Spanish had launched a preemptive attack on the French fort, St. Caroline. No fantasy of starting anew was ever realized without an armed advance guard, and bloody contention, as Derek Walcott's "The Fortunate Traveller" (1981) reminds us:

> Leaning on the hot rail, watching the hot sea,
> I saw them far off, kneeling on hot sand
> in the pious genuflections of the locust,
> as Ponce's armoured knees crush Florida
> to the funereal fragrance of white lilies.

On the pretty, shallow, turquoise green Matanzas River on the other side of a spit that faces out to the Atlantic, small children can wade without fear of rip currents or sharks. Overlooking it, though, is a stark coquina watch tower built in 1742 by the triumphant Spanish to guard St. Augustine upriver. You can take a ferry to it—to Rattlesnake Island, it's called—and climb the bastion overlooking the acres of wild marsh and ruffled water. It's the same landscape as centuries ago—black mangroves and sea grapes, sea oats and cactus, gopher turtles patiently tugging at tough, salty leaves while pelicans make their graceful sweeps across the shoreline.

Back in Gainesville, in 1854, a South Carolina plantation owner resettled with fifty-six slave laborers and built a homestead on the 1,500-acre Kanapaha Plantation. The Sea Island cotton failed to thrive, and Thomas Evans Haile lost the house to bankruptcy. It was repurchased by an affluent relative, who signed it over to Serena Chesnut Haile, Thomas's wife. Serena, mother to fifteen children (only one of whom didn't survive to adulthood), ran the plantation anew and diversified the crops (cowpeas, watermelon, scuppernongs), this time with success.

Here was another story about starting over. In the early twenty-first century, the plantation is a suburban development. The big house stands at a remove; after decades of neglect, it is now a museum dedicated to educating the public about the legacy of the Hailes and their enslaved men and women. There are sundry artifacts of nineteenth-century life—from pie safes to chamber pots—but the real attraction of the house, its claim to specialness, is its "talking walls."

There are over 12,500 words scribbled, graffiti-like, on most of the walls from eye level downward. The first notation was made by one of the children, writing his name in an upstairs storage nook in 1859. It seems as though the mistress of the house not only countenanced the practice but also contributed hundreds of notes, memos, and messages in her own hand, from recipes to inventories to a mysterious set of dates, found in her closet, which may have tracked her menstrual cycle. After she died and the house passed into the hands of her son, it stood mostly empty, used as a setting for his parties around the turn of the century.

Inspired by the graffiti of the past, the partygoers doodled and signed their names and commemorated the evening's guest list in the music parlor.

For Serena Haile, the walls were a memo pad, a diary, a household message board. In fact, she made her house an open book. In the Florida wilderness of the mid-nineteenth century, a family had to devise its own amusements. Serena's eccentricities didn't find expression in poetry—she was no Emily Dickinson, who scribbled lines on marginal bits of paper like envelope flaps and the backs of recipes between chores—although I did find this fragment of verse on her bedroom wall, where she and her husband exchanged messages:

> The shallows murmur
> But the depths are dumb

This is a misremembering of Sir Walter Raleigh: "Passions are likened best to floods and streams:/The shallows murmur, but the deeps are dumb" from "The Silent Lover," written in the late sixteenth century. The poem refutes the idea that love could be put into words:

> So, when affections yield discourse, it seems
> The bottom is but shallow whence they come.
> They that are rich in words, in words discover
> That they are poor in that which makes a lover.

This is a suitably romantic apology for a spouse who might have struggled with verbal expressions of affection. And then, further astonished, I found a verse of Lord Byron's, from "The Giaour":

> But love itself could never pant
> For all that beauty sighs to grant
> With half the fervour hate bestows
> Upon the last embrace of foes.

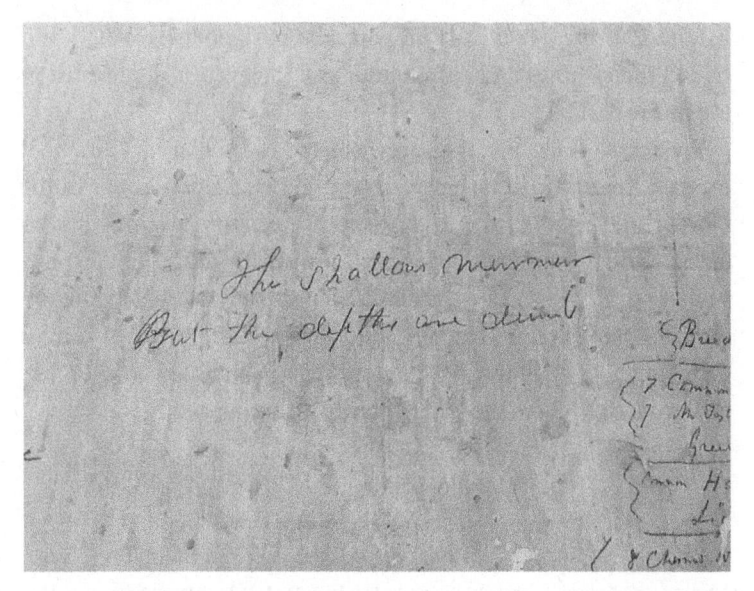

Lines from Sir Walter Raleigh's "The Silent Lover," Haile Homestead at Kanapaha Plantation, Gainesville, FL

What was *this* stanza doing in the marriage chamber, I wondered! But whatever the privations of life in this lonely settlement, Raleigh and Byron—and probably other poets—were here. This was the same sea dog Raleigh who had created, and lost, the colony at Roanoke. Byron's "The Giaour" is one of his popular "oriental tales" and features a knight who loves and suffers in a far-flung, foreign war zone.

Poetry seemed to flourish in crevices and nooks in Florida, like the resurrection fern in live oaks.

*

In an essay on Robert Frost, W. H. Auden observed that

> we want a poem to be beautiful, that is to say, a verbal earthly paradise, a timeless world of pure play, which gives us delight precisely because of its contrast to our historical existence with

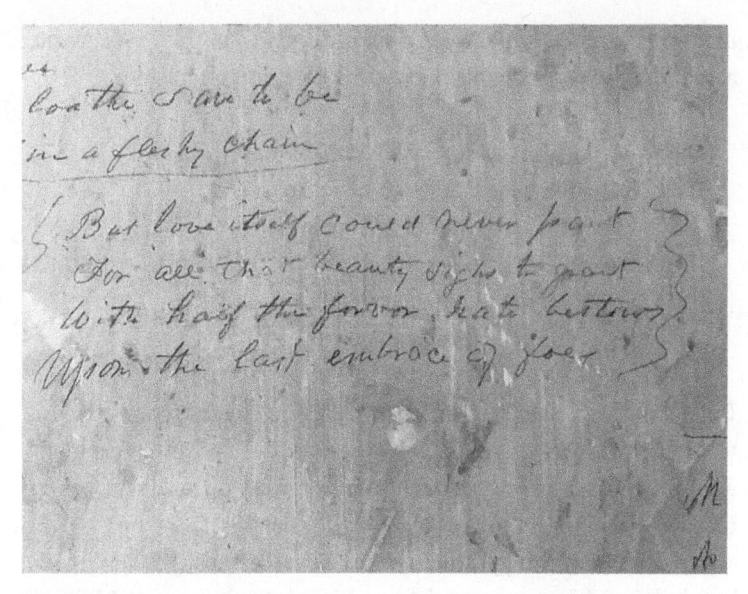

Lines from Lord Byron's "The Giaour," Haile Homestead at Kanapaha Plantation, Gainesville, FL

> all its insoluble problems and inescapable suffering; at the same time we want a poem to be true, that is to say, to provide us with some kind of revelation about our life which will show us what life is really like and free us from self-enchantment and deception, and a poet cannot bring us any truth without introducing into his poetry the problematic, the painful, the disorderly, the ugly.[6]

The effect of formal beauty, he writes, is "evil to the degree that beauty is taken, not as analogous to, but identical with goodness, so that the artist regards himself or is regarded by others as God, the pleasure of beauty being taken for the joy of Paradise, and the conclusion drawn that, since all is well in the work of art, all is well in history."[7]

Frost himself thought that style "is that which indicates how the writer takes himself and what he is saying."[8] Frost understood that literary style is personal style; Sir John Davies, in the 1590s, wrote a sonnet in which language is the invisible dressing itself:

> The sacred Muse that first made love divine
> hath made him naked and without attire
> but I will clothe him with this pen of mine
> that all the world his fashion shall admire
> his hat of hope, this band of beauty fine
> his cloak of craft, his doublet of desire.[9]

But Frost goes even further than that: He suggests that a stylist writes as if with a split consciousness. He has a subterranean awareness of his own seriousness or absurdity or both, even as he directs our attention to the subject matter at hand.

Frost was no stranger to Florida; he passed through Gainesville regularly on his way to and from his winter home near Miami, Pencil Pines, and he spent time, too, in Key West, where he and Wallace Stevens met up at the Casa Marina hotel. At least one of their gruff exchanges made literary history:

> STEVENS: The trouble with you is you write about things.
> FROST: The trouble with you is you write about bric-a-brac.[10]

Yet the landscape made no great impression on his poetry, as the northern landscapes of New Hampshire and Vermont did. Frost's own plain style was forged in the study of Latin and Greek; the plain style is a classical style, based on the austere, chiseled lines of the ancients. In 1939, Yvor Winters, advocating vociferously for the plain style and against the ornate "Petrarchists" (after Francesco Petrarch, the fourteenth-century Renaissance poet and scholar—a major influence on Dante and the Provençal Troubadours), described his neglected school thus: "a theme usually broad, simple, and obvious, even tending toward the proverbial, but usually a theme of some importance, humanly speaking; a feeling restrained to the minimum required by the subject; a rhetoric restrained to a similar minimum, the poet being interested in his rhetoric as a means of stating his matter as economically as possible, and not, as are the Petrarchans, in the pleasures of rhetoric for its own sake."[11] Thom Gunn was Winters's student in the 1950s at Stanford and shared with his teacher a lifelong passion for Renaissance poetry. Discussing style in his essay "Enmeshed with Time," he explained the two dominant Tudor styles as ones of "discrimination" and "abundance": "C. S. Lewis called them Drab and Golden; Yvor Winters Plain and Ornate; and others have given them other names. In describing them as the poetries of discrimination and abundance I am trying to recognize that the styles are not always or necessarily in mutual opposition. Now they may be distinct, but now they may be continuous one with the other."[12] Could we update our terms to the *Temperate* and the *Tropical*?

Only one style gets singled out for vilification: *prolix. Purple.* Is there a term of disapprobation for its opposite? For though the abundant, golden, tropical style gestures toward Paradise, it also signifies decadence, indulgence. *Expensiveness.* The plain style ("economical") gets the job done without fuss. Without calling attention to itself. It's more serious: it recognizes that we have no time to waste. The plain, or drab, or discriminating, or temperate style is keenly aware of death. *Timor mortis conturbat me.* The tropical style is shocking, almost insulting, in its insistence on fecundity.

Is style an attitude toward life and death, then?

*

The first point of contention between the styles was vocabulary. One believed in either abundance of vocabulary or its opposite.

Winters's foremost precursor in these style wars was "plain" Ben Jonson. In his satire *Poetaster* (1601), a bad versifier called Crispinus accosts the great Horace on the streets of ancient

Rome and tries to impress him with his terrible works (which he can barely remember, stumbling badly through equally bad lines); Horace tries to get away from this "Land-Remora" as soon as possible. Crispinus is tried for calumny against Horace in a tribunal consisting of Caesar, Virgil, Maecenas, Propertius, and Ovid—the whole gang from the golden age—and his punishment is to take pills that will make him vomit up his offending vocabulary:

> CRI. O——
>   TIB. How now, Crispinus?
>   CRI. O, I am sick—— ... O—retrograde—reciprocal—Incubus.
>   CÆS. What's that, Horace?
>   HOR. Retrograde, and reciprocal Incubus are come up.
>   GAL. Thanks be to Jupiter.
>   CRIS. O—glibbery—lubrical—defunct—O—
>   HOR. Well said; here's some store.
>   VIR. What are they?
>   HOR. Glibbery, lubrical, and defunct.
>   GAL. O, they came up easie.
>   CRIS. O—O—
>   TIB. What's that?
>   HOR. Nothing yet.
>   CRIS. Magnificate.
>   MEC. Magnificate? That came up somewhat hard.
>   HOR. I. What chear, Crispinus?
>   CRIS. O, I shall cast up my—spurious—snotteries—
>   HOR. Good. Again.
>   CRIS. Chilblain'd—O—O—clumsie—
>   HOR. That clumsie stuck terribly.
>   MEC. What's all that, Horace?
>   HOR. Spurious, snotteries, chilblain'd, clumsie.

TIB. O Jupiter.
GAL. Who would have thought there should ha' been such a deal of Filth in a Poet?
CRIS. O—barmy froth—
CÆS. What's that?
CRIS.—Puffie—inflate—turgidous—ventositous.
HOR. Barmy froth, puffie, inflate, turgidous, and ventositous are come up.
TIB. O terrible windy words.
GAL. A sign of a windy Brain.
CRIS. O—Oblatrant—furibund—fatuate—strenuous—
HOR. Here's a deal; oblatrant, furibund, fatuate, strenuous.
CÆS. Now all's come up, I trow. What a Tumult he had in his Belly!

"Tumult," in Jonson's time, was a word used for public mobs and insurrection. But in this tumult is an uproarious comic riff, a sly appreciation of ingenuity and hyperbole. Freed from utilitarian use value, the Latinate words devolve into nonsense syllables, heterogeneous, musical, and melismatic—belonging to the set of speech acts that articulate emotion rather than thought: exclamations, oaths, profanities, obscenities, sighs, and grunts. Not only is this list fun to read (and dramatize), but also it is cathartic. It is a safe form of misrule, like most entertainment, in which excess exuberance is vented but no one gets hurt.

There was a xenophobic subtext to the late-sixteenth-century style wars (the "poetomachia"). One of Winters's favorite neglected poets, George Gascoigne, advocated monosyllabic words ("the more monosyllables that you use, the truer Englishman you shall seeme").[13] In 1594, Thomas Wilson published *The Art of Rhetorique*, advocating "one manner" of English, plain rather than "outlandish." The outland in outlandish was mostly France. French, along with Italian and Latin loan words, threatened to make of English a "gallimaufry or hodge-podge," warned Edmund Spenser.[14]

This culinary metaphor gives way to metaphors of promiscuity or miscegenation; in its impurity, language is "wanton." The poet Thomas Nashe (1567–1601) accused his ideological enemies of "supplanting and setting aside the true children of the English, and suborning inkehorne changlings in their steade."[15] French, in particular, was associated with "gallantry," that is, libertinism, as the euphemism for syphilis—"the French disease"—illustrates. (It was also called the "à la mode disease," which gives new meaning, perhaps, to Francophile Wallace Stevens's "emperor of ice cream"; the French, meanwhile, called it "the Italian disease.") In the mid-eighteenth century, Samuel Johnson reprised this argument in the preface to his *Dictionary*, inveighing, "Our language, for almost a century, has by the concurrence of many causes been gradually departing from its *Teutonick* character, and deviating towards a *Gallick* structure and phraseology, from which it ought to be our endeavor to recall it, by making our ancient vollumes the groundwork of stile."[16]

Nor were neologisms permissible to the plain stylists. Renaissance poet Samuel Daniel condemned "forging strange and unusual words."[17] Yet Shakespeare gave us *alligator, bedroom, critic, eyeball, gossip, kissing, lonely, manager, zany*. Robert Herrick invented *lautitious, repululation, circumspangle, tardidation, discruciate, progermination, circumgyration, superlast*. Samuel Taylor Coleridge gave us *psychosomatic, neuropathology, intensify*. John Keats contributed *surgy, palely, soother,* and *adventuresome*. In 1820, a reviewer complained that Keats's work was "unintelligible" and urged him to "avoid coining new words."[18] But he was under the influence of the writer and editor Leigh Hunt, who believed, as Lucasta Miller puts it, "to make free with the English language" was inexorably tied to "belief in political, and indeed sexual, freedom."[19]

Plainness is equated with straight-shooting, and ornateness supposedly dissimulates. But all verbal persuasion entails a performance. Evolutionary biologists invented the term "honest signals" to describe the unfakeability of so-called "costly" ornaments like peacock tails. So if there is an "honest signal" in poetry, it is located in the ornate style, which wears its colors on its sleeve. Plain style is the equivalent of biological camouflage. Apparent simplicity is shrewd. It disavows ornament, but it only pretends to be disinterested, uninvested, or uninvolved in its terseness.

*

Whatever you want to call these styles—plain or drab or temperate; ornate or golden or Petrarchist or abundant or tropical—the word "ornament" is key: its deployment or its lack is a statement of value.

In his memoir, *A Different Person* (1993), James Merrill gives an account of his travels in Europe as a young man, a journey that put him in a long line of poets whose education culminated in the necessary lived experience of Italy and Greece, where poetry as we know it began. It was as though the eruptions of Etna or Vesuvius birthed raw forms, sonnets and canzones, sestinas and ottava rimas free for export into English, where they would be fashioned with fresh wit. This was true for Geoffrey Chaucer, for Thomas Wyatt, for Byron, for Percy Shelley, for Pound. Merrill had the means to adapt himself to this tradition—the means and the wisdom.

One of the most memorable people he met on his travels was the Dante scholar Irma Brandeis, then in her forties: "She has the lofty bearing and principles of those ladies with garlands or a musical instrument, to whom sestinas were written in the dolce stil nuovo, ladies quick to chastise the unvirtuous, stern in spirit, gentle in heart and speech."[20] She "comes to lunch in Rome, bringing us a book by a poet whose name neither Claude nor I have heard—Eugenio Montale."[21] Brandeis had been Montale's lover and confidante, the Clytia of his poetry and probable muse of the great twentieth-century poem "The Eel," about an animal that comes to stand for the underground circulation of life, love, and knowledge. While Merrill sat tongue-tied, Brandeis and his partner Claude Fredericks hit it off, chatting enthusiastically "about Aquinas or 'difficult ornament' in medieval rhetoric."[22] What was "difficult ornament"? I wondered. So I went looking.

The Princeton Encyclopedia of Poetry and Poetics: "ORNAMENT. An accessory or embellishment, an element added to some object. It may or may not contribute to the structure or effective functioning of that object, but it must have some kind of independent interest, and most often this is an aesthetic one. An o. adorns, or adds charm, splendor, or beauty to the object; it fascinates by its refinement or exoticness; or it challenges perception and stimulates comprehension by its intricacy or grotesqueness....All cultures have used o.... Classical medieval and Renaissance theorists spent much time identifying and classifying the 'flowers,' 'gems,' and 'colors' of expression. Distinctions were made between schemes and tropes, figures of speech and figures of thought, and 'difficult' and easy o.... Florid style...since classical times has been known as the 'Asiatic.'"

I did a Google search, which led me to very few hits regarding the twelfth-century poetic rhetorician Geoffrey of Vinsauf (or Geoffrey the Englishman), whose *Poetria nova*, a two thousand–line poem based on Horace's *Ars Poetica*, explicates "difficult ornament" with examples: tropes, metaphors, conceits; the art of using one one thing to speak of another in a one-to-one correspondence. Elsewhere, I read, word play, stanza linking, and complex rhyme scheme are included under difficult ornament. Difficult ornament, I conclude, names the quality I love so much in Wallace Stevens, Marianne Moore, James Merrill, Harry Mathews—the word play, the labyrinthine syntax, the patterning, and most of all the metaphors that, with tendrils invading every part of speech, blossom into full-blown metonyms. This is the most transformative element in a poet's repertoire. It dissolves the boundaries between beings and between the world and the imagination. Difficult ornament is the Sir John Davies poem:

> Grief for a girdle shall about him twine;
> His points of pride, his eyelet-holes of ire,
> His hose of hate, his codpiece of conceit,
> His stockings of stern strife, his shirt of shame;
> His garters of vain glory, gay and slight,
> His pantofles of passions I will frame;
> Pumps of presumption shall adorn his feet,
> And socks of sullenness exceeding sweet.[23]

Here is difficult ornament in all its wit (sullen socks, of course, can't possibly smell sweet—even if "feet" is a pun on metrical language). It effectively delineates all the features of a personified Love—giving shading to its complex of emotions, including lust and pride and envy and resentment.

Merrill was our foremost practitioner of difficult ornament in recent decades. But "difficult" suggests obscurity; Merrill wasn't a particularly obscure poet. His themes were love, domesticity, friendship, and their survival beyond death. An exemplary poem of difficult ornament might be the poem he wrote for his mother at the end of his life, titled (fittingly for my "ornament") "Pearl." He reminisced about the precious stone that mesmerized a small son: "at home in the hollow/Of his mother's throat: the real, deepwater thing." Mer = mère (the French pun on sea and mother is never foreign to Merrill). And the grain, the mote, of irritation that prompts the oyster to secrete the nacre—that irritation, too, is natural, even between son and mother. The nacre is the essence of art: the polish that ameliorates our disappointment at life. In the end, our narrator, who teaches a seminar in capital-L Loss, takes his class to a "revival" of a film, *Perles de la Couronne*: "The hero has tracked down/His prize."

> He's holding forth, that summer night,
> At the ship's rail, all suavity and wit,
> Gem swaying like a pendulum
> From his fing—oops! To soft bubble-blurred harpstring
> Arpeggios regaining depths (man the camera, follow)
> Where an unconscious world, my yawning oyster,
> Shuts on it.

The metonym dances in this poem: From the remembered mother's pearl to the pearl at the remembered film's end, Merrill juggles variations on the notion of bringing precious things up from the depths (whence they will drop again one day). His final pun on the proverbial "the world is your oyster" precludes any elegiac bathos, but the shut oyster is, at last, a coffin. And stepping back from the poem as a semantic vehicle, you suddenly realize: The mirroring stanzas make a concrete image. On the page is an oyster-poem with a hinge, and the rhymes make a palindrome. The first, middle, and last lines rhyme in a way that condenses the entire poem:

> admit (opening line)
> of grit (middle line)
> Shuts on it. (closing line)

"Admit" even reveals its double meaning, once you double back on the beginning of the poem: at first meaning "to confess," it ends up meaning "to let in" (as in letting in the irritating grit). And yet, for all the wit and cleverness of the poem, it is not merely admiration one feels on the whole. Difficult ornament seems designed to elicit a mixture of feelings. There is poignancy cut with sad mirth, fitting for the sixty-eight-year-old poet, dying of AIDS, writing to the mother who will outlive him by five years.

*

"Difficult" ornament might suggest not only obscurity but also sententiousness. Yet one could write a comic poem of difficult ornament, like Merrill's tribute to Elizabeth Bishop, "The Victor Dog":

> Bix to Buxtehude to Boulez.
> The little white dog on the Victor label
> Listens long and hard as he is able.
> It's all in a day's work, whatever plays.
>
> From judgment, it would seem, he has refrained.
> He even listens earnestly to Bloch,
> Then builds a church upon our acid rock.
> He's man's—no—he's the Leiermann's best friend,
>
> Or would be if hearing and listening were the same.
> Does he hear? I fancy he rather smells
> Those lemon-gold arpeggios in Ravel's
> "Les jets d'eau du palais de ceux qui s'aiment."

The world-renowned icon of the Victor dog, with its motto "His Master's Voice," has a backstory of its own: it was trademarked by British, German, and Japanese corporations over the decades since its first incarnation, as an 1899 oil painting by a Frenchman living in England named Francis Barraud. Nipper, the original dog in the painting, was a Jack Russell mix born in Bristol. Barraud reminisced: "It is difficult to say how the idea came to me beyond that fact that it suddenly occurred to me that to have my dog listening to the phonograph, with an intelligent and rather puzzled expression, and call it 'His Master's Voice' would make an excellent subject. We had a phonograph and I often noticed how puzzled he was to make out where the voice came from. It certainly was the happiest thought I ever had."[24] Ironically, Barraud had a difficult time selling the image initially: he was told that people wouldn't understand what the dog was doing, because, according to the Edison Bell Company, "dogs don't listen to phonographs."[25]

But this very quality is probably what struck Merrill: its incongruity allows the imagination to leap into action, filling in the logical gap between the image and ordinary experience. And at any rate, the "intelligent and rather puzzled expression" caused by the unnatural contraption really ought to be intelligible to anyone confronting the cosmos in a technological age—it's easy to see ourselves in the bemused dog. Above all, there was humor in the image, mixed with an appeal to the child buried in us—like a cartoon dog or stuffed animal. And it spoke to art as entertainment. Merrill's poem, which enacts and comments on musical performance, is meant, first, to entertain.

This lightness was something Merrill shared with his idol Elizabeth Bishop, who also courted and deflected pathos in poems like "The Filling Station" or "The Man-Moth." In fact, Bishop conceived of "The Man-Moth" after seeing the word—a misprint for "mammoth"—in the newspaper and ran away with the idea. Like the Victor dog, the Man-Moth was a comically low-brow stand-in for the artist in the modern world; he played with his own teardrop like a magician's toy.

Having dedicated the poem to Elizabeth Bishop, Merrill started in the key of B: "Bix to Buxtehude to Boulez." Much was encoded in that first line: from the twentieth-century jazz cornetist to the early baroque choral composer and back to a twentieth-century powerhouse of experimental composed music, each name is an emblem for a wide range of musical expression: in the second stanza, "acid rock" is rhymed with modern Swiss American composer Ernest Bloch to underscore the point. All of which serve a further point: that the dog is pure obedience; he does not exercise "taste." Paradoxically, the artist's "work" is to actively listen, but be passive in his judgments toward the world. The balanced, rhyming *abba* iambic pentameter quatrains enact the seesaw between "work" and "play," action and passivity.

Work and play is the dominant binary, but the other kind of doubling Merrill engages in happens at the level of the word, with his relentless punning. To pun is to make deliberate use of a word's over- and undertones, exploiting its full "resonance," to borrow a metaphor from acoustics. To "[build] a church upon our acid rock" puns both on Christ's anointing of St. Peter and on the inherent instability of acid rock (limestone) landscapes. (Think, too, of the crypto-spiritual grandeur of acid rock—Merrill's double entendres really mean what they say.) Then he puns on "man's best friend" with a reference to "Der Leiermann," the last piece in Franz Schubert's "Winterreise" song cycle, based on a poem by Wilhelm Mueller, which addresses a cold, hungry organ grinder whose music falls on deaf ears and growling street dogs, to which the Victor dog provides a contrast in nobility.

Was Merrill suggesting that, along with the alertness and receptivity of the dog, one must have a nose for hunting allusions? Some readers object to the demand that they rummage outside the poem—in dictionaries or encyclopedias—to catch the full range of meaning, but Merrill suggests that's not entirely necessary, at least at a first reading: "I fancy he rather smells/Those lemon-gold arpeggios in Ravel's/'Les jets d'eau du palais de ceux qui s'aiment.'" That is, the sheer epicurean pleasure of hearing the notes—in this case, the rhythm and pictures of words like "lemon-gold arpeggios" or the melodious syllables of French—gratifies the senses, which is where the real excitement is. The "full range of meaning" (as if that were something we could ever truly arrive at!) can wait.

For several stanzas, the poem serves as a playlist with corresponding metaphors. Schumann's "tall willow hit/by lightning" alludes to the thunderous chords that begin and end his Piano Concerto op. 54; Bach's "eternal boxwood mazes," besides punning on his name, capture the labyrinthine structure of baroque canons and fugues, while calypso is figured as a kind of intoxicant, appropriate to festivities. The range of experience is there: happiness, love, suffering, and death. (The pun on "adamant needles" refers to not only the record needle but "thorns also and thistles" that God promises to Adam after the Fall.) The dog continues to be stoic, facing all situations with the same equanimity: "He was taught as a puppy not to flinch." Notice how quickly—almost in passing—Merrill suggests that the attentive, sympathetic observation of suffering (Lear's existential anguish, love's treachery, murder, war) might effect a change, that is, progress, in "nature": "Can nature change in him? Nothing's impossible."

But wisdom is dispensed fleetingly in the poem's comic universe. The final image is one adapted from the *Paradiso*, the climax of Dante's *Divine Comedy*. If the classic definition of comedy is a story with a happy ending, Merrill suggests that something quite grand—victory, even—awaits the artist-dog. At the volta, after the seventh stanza, "the last chord fades" and the Victor dog sleeps on the "still-warm" gramophone as on a rug before a hearth, dreaming of starring in his own (apocryphal) opera named after a small constellation, Canis Minor—"lesser dog." This is a convenient segue to the image of the starry cosmos. Just as the phonograph spindle "gives rise to harmonies beyond belief," in Dante's universe there is a "music of the spheres" arising from the sun, moon, and planets' harmonization with one another based on resonances, determined by numerical ratios—a theory that originated with Pythagoras and expanded its influence through Boethius's treatise *De Musica*. The spindle would be likened to the earth's axis, which runs up to the Pole Star, likened to the diamond in the record needle. Finally, the planets' orbits would be the grooves in the record. Dante's climactic imagery lies behind Merrill's:

> But now my will and my desire, like
> wheels revolving

> with an even motion, were turning with
> the Love that moves the sun and all the
> other stars.

Redeeming the Leiermann, our Victor dog, passive listener and dreamer, turns the derogatory "dog's life" into a triumph with a "cast of stars."

There may be one more buried allusion here, and that is to another famous dog in English literature. It is Alexander Pope's "Epigram Engraved on the Collar of a Dog which I Gave to His Royal Highness":

> I am Sir Highness' dog at Kew;
> pray tell me sir, whose dog are you?

Pope sent this to the Prince of Wales with a puppy from his dog Bounce's litter. I think of James Merrill in this season of frustrated love, asking himself, tongue-in-cheek, Whose dog are you? and then writing his poem for his adored mentor, affirming their shared vocation.

"Difficult ornament" keeps heartbreak at bay. Merrill wrote "The Victor Dog" in the fall of 1969, in Nambé Pueblo, New Mexico, outside Santa Fe. It was there that he rented an adobe cottage for some months to be close to a painter friend, David McIntosh. The romance he was trying to kindle kept faltering back into friendship, and though McIntosh served as a companion and guide to the geology and lore of the Southwest, his affections lay elsewhere. Merrill, who claimed never to have spent a night alone (he was never without a partner, if not an entourage), found himself disappointed in love again, soon after a previous relationship, in Greece, had left him heartbroken. Alone with books and records under extravagantly starry skies, in the atmospheric acuteness at elevation six thousand feet, Merrill fell back on the wisdom of his forty-three years. He wrote wittily, poignantly, and resignedly about the philosophical consolation of art, in his most exuberant style—a style, as Gunn would say, of abundance, or of difficult ornament.

*

Instead of calling the style of my Florida poets that of abundance, or difficult ornament, or even tropical (Florida is, strictly speaking, subtropical), I will opt for something more creaturely: the peacock style.

I love peacocks. Catullus, Sir Philip Sidney, Lord Byron...yet the actual bird frightens me as much as it fascinates me. I remember in particular a pair that haunted the grounds of St. John the Divine Cathedral. When I lived for three years in Morningside Heights at the turn of the millennium, in a building called the Laureate, I would stroll there to sit with a cup of coffee and a notebook in the rose garden, or the Bible garden. One of the peacocks was what is called "leucistic," from the Greek *leukos*, white. If Pavo Phasianidae in all their iridescent glory weren't striking enough, the white peacock was even more of a marvel to me: ghostlike, eerie, whether it crossed my path in sunlight or sought the shade of the cloister. A friend who lived closer to the cathedral complained about the shrieking, and one day I got to hear it for myself. I was holding my friend's newborn baby, debuted to a small cohort in her thirteenth-floor apartment, when the peacock cry announced itself. Not very long after that, I was pregnant myself.

"What eyelashes," the optometrist said, many years later, as she was measuring my son for new glasses. "Men have more beautiful eyelashes; it's so unfair. It's called the peacock effect." The peacock effect in poetry has proved a durable survival strategy, though it has its detractors. (Call them "pavophobic" readers.) One day in early spring, I received a letter from my friend in Athens. She had written something for me—we were in the habit of exchanging poem epistles—and it was a poem about peacocks, which overran her rented weekend house on an island in the Saronic Gulf. She enclosed one of the feathers. It was from her that I learned that you shouldn't invite peacocks onto your property (Hera's bird: they portend adultery), but I had no husband to peacuckold. I turned over the feather delightedly.

Peacocks have increasingly become nuisances in Florida, I learned. One day, my sons saw one in our backyard and we congregated at the window, mouths agape. It seemed to be missing its tail. Yet I took it as a good omen anyway, as I was about to depart for an overseas trip. Everything went well with the trip, but the peacock never returned.

Florida has a peacock character. The starburst shapes of its palms and palmettoes, the turquoise of its forested inland springs, the emerald of its gulf and ocean shores, the aquamarine of its swimming pools. The ersatz architecture, the blinding stuccos and fountains, the canary yellows and neon pinks of Miami. Palm Beach. Naples and Venice. All fabled, bejeweled destinations. Bijoux. The peacock is hung with ornaments from the tips of its crest to the tips of its fantail feathers. In Europe, it appeared on royal menus, broiled and served with a garnish of lemon and flowers.

Where peacocks and other creatures are concerned, ornament is a technical description. Biological ornament (whence we get our honest signals) is a hotbed of theories. Most of us are blessed with one or two ornaments. A peacock has multiple ornaments, which demands an explanation. There's a "redundant signal" hypothesis, in which the redundancy of ornaments points to different aspects of fitness. But what if the ornament has an ambivalent character? The tail, for instance, may be beautiful, but it is also an encumbrance that could possibly put a bird's life in danger. For this, a "handicap selection" was suggested, reasoning that a female could see that the male thrived even with the handicap, so his genes were desirable. Camouflage, like plain style, may cheat the eye; bright feathers announce they have nothing to hide.

If poetic ornament is analogous to biological ornament, so lexical diversity can be analogous to species diversity. If nature loves abundance, why not language?

Just a few miles from my house, a man was found dead in a corral where he kept a cassowary. He was sliced open by her four-inch talons and bled out through a severed artery in his arm. Suddenly everyone was googling cassowary: a bird that grows up to six feet tall, 160 pounds, covered in long black feathers, from whose body rises an iridescent blue neck and a head crested not with feathers, but with keratin. Long, red wattles hang from either side of its sour-looking face. The bird's extravagant appearance is more monstrous than beautiful. A few weeks after the killing, the bird was put up for sale at the Gulf Coast Livestock Auction, along with other animals from the man's menagerie: five ring-tailed and ruffed lemurs, nineteen macaws, twenty-six marmosets, and an emu.

Each of the poets discussed in this small treatise displayed their difficult ornaments with panache. Stevens flaunted a rococo vocabulary so inclusive that its French and Spanish words become naturalized in his poetry. Moore, Merrill, and Mathews invented difficult stanzas and forms; Merrill was adventurous with rhyme, and Bishop deployed metonyms, as well as forms and rhymes, in novel ways. She also had the rare gift of finding original similes—the ornament most likely to give us the shock of the unexpected. All strove to transfer emotional difficulty onto structures that could bear the load. All of them touched on the abundance of form in Florida (prolific, proliferative, prolix in plants and animals) and made emblems of its flora, fauna, springs, and gales. They also knew there were deadly aspects to Florida: pollution and predation. But it also made them dwell on—if not in—Paradise.

2

Wallace Stevens

Green Cocoanut Ice Cream

> "He also sent Holly objects to educate her in the earth's richness: one year, palmetto fronds; the next, a baby alligator that she could show at school and that later, he wisely noted, could be taken to the Elizabeth Park greenhouse, where it would be able to survive the North's weather." —Joan Richardson, *Wallace Stevens: The Later Years*[1]

On the one hand, the elements of a physical peacock: a man over six feet tall, over two hundred pounds in his middle years, who liked to cut a figure. "I'm not sure that on occasions he doesn't go to bed with a silk hat," remarked a fellow member of New York's Century Club in the 1950s.[2] His wife responded: "I don't think so. I think he finds it just very difficult. He would like to relax very much, but he finds it very difficult. You must forgive him." She was closer to the mark. Wallace Stevens's colleagues at Hartford Insurance Company agreed that he didn't have friends.[3] He lived in a spacious manor with his reclusive wife, Elsie, in a cold marriage; their hobby was gardening, and they gardened separate plots. He was diligent in his work, refined in his tastes, and quietly authored some of the most sublime American poetry from the first half of the twentieth century, very little of it wielding the second half of the century's favorite pronoun, "I." He deflected readers who would presume too much intimacy. He found it just very difficult.

On the other hand, for almost twenty years beginning in 1922, Stevens used annual business trips to Florida lasting two weeks to a month to escape the strictures of his decorous Connecticut life and his own exacting temperament. The man who purportedly had no friends in Hartford maintained a set in the South, where he also ate and drank with sybaritic gusto (at home, his wife watched his diet and made him teetotal—thus his lavish spending on tea from Ceylon during the Depression). His boon companion of thirty years, with whom he traveled to Miami and Key West and a tony fishing club in Long Key, was judge Arthur Powell of Atlanta, a senior law partner in the firm of Little & Powell, which did business with Hartford Insurance.

Charles O'Dowd, an underwriter at Stevens's firm, reminisced about his old colleague, whose legal correspondence struck him as "beautifully written." "It gave you quite a vocabulary, because he would go after a precise, even though remote, meaning. The guy I saw using the big dictionary in the law library more than anyone else was Wallace Stevens."[4] He also remembered the "delightful" letters that went back and forth between Stevens and Powell, who was his counsel in bond-claims cases in the South: "The question came up, what he should wear before the Supreme Court. Powell said, 'I finally dusted off the swallow-tail coat which is indigenous to a great many Southern lawyers and which, when I was presented with the same problem when I was presented to the King and Queen of England, I dared to wear.'"[5] Two peacocks, then, trawling the Florida Straits in a yacht, fishing for tarpon, tuna, or sailfish; or sunbathing at the Casa Marina Hotel in Key West. In 1923, Stevens wrote Elsie from Long Key: "This evening we had doves on toast for dinner. Wild doves are a delicacy in the South. I can't say that they exceed anything else I ever tasted.... The beauty of this place is indescribable. This morning the sea was glittering gold and intense deep blue. When it grew cloudy later the sea turned to green and black."[6] He admitted that there was a preponderance of mosquitoes, the only flaw in paradise.

His biographer Peter Brazeau's description of "railroad executives, bankers and lawyers" on their "masculine idyll" sounds like nothing so much as the revelers in Preston Sturges's *Palm Beach Story*, where plucky Claudette Colbert relies on the kindness of comical businessmen making merry on the Florida Special.[7] Stevens "liked to imagine himself as one of the boys. He particularly liked the camaraderie of Powell's circle because the Georgia men of affairs he met at the camp roughed it in style, whether feasting on doves and haunch of venison in a club member's private railroad car or cruising along the Florida coast aboard the yacht of Powell's law partner."[8]

Stevens came to see Powell as a literary fellow traveler and confidante. As a child, Powell accompanied his lawyer father to courts all over "red clay country"—where Georgia, Florida, and Alabama meet—and was himself admitted to the bar by the age of eighteen. He was a "gifted raconteur," a treasury of regional idioms, "spokesman for his land."[9] Stevens was fascinated, both as a Yankee who was increasingly interested in his Pennsylvania Dutch roots and as a poet who had begun a draft of a poem called "From the Journal of Crispin," in which his central thesis is that "man is the intelligence of his soil." His alter ego, Crispin, started to take on some of Judge Powell's colors. Stevens changed a line of the poem in Powell's honor: "The man in Georgia waking among pines/Should be pine-spokesman" had originally been "the man from Mississippi." Powell, in turn, was an ardent follower of Stevens's verse: "In February, 1935, we were at Key West again; and his poem 'Mozart [1935]'...was forming in his mind....I now have in my possession a scrap of brown paper, a piece of a heavy envelope, with this written on it in his handwriting":

> ses hurlements,
> ses chucuotments, ses ricaments.
> its hoo-hoo-hoo
> Its shoo-shoo-shoo, its ric-nic.[10]

And written on hotel stationery in Tampa in 1934, he remembered:

> The humming bird is king among
> humming birds;
> But Vitis is a castor bean
> And a ticket seller.[11]

"Vitus is a small junction point on the ACL Railway just out of Tampa," Powell explained. "And he gave a full description of it."[12]

Through Powell, Stevens met another history-obsessed Florida lawyer named Philip May. May offered to show Stevens "one or two places of interest to poets near Jacksonville which you haven't seen—Fort Clinch, at the entrance of Fernandina harbor, and just beyond, some sand dunes covered with the most remarkable and lovely wind-blown trees I have ever seen; St. Mary's, an old English settlement...where there is a country hotel, which makes oyster stew from unwashed oysters."[13] May took Stevens down the Palm Coast to Ormond Beach and to various sites around the St. John's River.

It was also Philip May who took Wallace Stevens to dinner at Marjorie Rawlings's house in Cross Creek in 1936. Stevens was on a strict diet—doctor's orders—which May warned Rawlings about. According to her memoir, *Cross Creek Cookery*, "I planned my best baked-in-sherry ham for the rest of the company, and wracked my brains for a method of making lean meat a delicacy. I decided to prepare the heart of a Boston pot roast of beef in an individual casserole, with sherry....He began on his beef, looked over at the clove-stuck ham, and announced that he would partake not only of that, but of all the other rich dishes on the table."[14] The way Philip May remembered it, Stevens "actually picked up his food and threw it over by the fireplace, then ate what everybody else ate."[15]

Stevens was evidently gratified by the dinner: "Mrs. Rawlings is a very remarkable woman in her own right as distinct from her literary right; and I look forward to seeing her again one of these days."[16]

From the start, Florida refreshed Wallace Stevens's senses and returned him to a Crusoe-like innocence, allowing him to rebuild his imagination from the ground up. Here, he is writing to his wife Elsie in 1916 from Miami for the first time:

> This is a jolly place—joli. It is alive. It is beautiful, too.... When I got here at midnight last night, the air was like pulp. But there is a constant wind that keeps stirring it up.... The town is situated on a bay which is separated from the sea beyond by a narrow beach. The beach is deserted at this season.... The houses are not pretentious. Their grounds are full of oleanders as large as orchard trees, groups of hibiscus, resembling holly-hocks, strange trumpet-vines, royal palms, cocoanut-palms full of cocoanuts, which litter the ground, orange and grape-fruit trees, mangoes in bloom, bougainvillea, castor-beans, etc. etc. You soon grow accustomed to the palms. The soil is utterly different from ours. It seems to be all sand covered with sparse grass and the surrounding jungle. After all, the important thing in Florida is the sun. It is as hot as a coal in the day-time. It goes down rather abruptly, with little twilight. Then the trade winds quickly blow the heat away and leave the air pulpy but cool.[17]

He tells her it is one of the most delightful places he has ever seen. Then in 1922, beholding the Keys for the first time (with Powell and company): "This is one of the choicest places I have ever been to." He describes the soil again, Crispin's motto incipient in his avid noticing: "The ground is white coral broken up, as white as this paper, dazzling in the sunshine.... The place is a a paradise—midsummer weather, the sky brilliantly clear and intensely blue, the sea blue and green beyond what you have ever seen."[18] Had Stevens lived to fly over Florida, he could have perceived the whiteness of Florida's ground-coquina roads from the air at night by the light of a full moon. They glow like veins of phosphor.

While Stevens's letters to Elsie attest to Florida's endless ability to flabbergast him, his Florida poems are an ecstasy of golden green: they are the odes that Adam would have declaimed in Eden. There is "Fabliau of Florida," "O, Florida, Venereal Soil," "Indian River," the "immense dew" of "Nomad Exquisite," whose key word "nomad" comes from the Greek *nomas*, "roaming in search of pasture." Later, the poems would turn elegiac: "A Farewell to Florida," "The Idea of Order at Key West," "A Fish-Scale Sunrise."

A fabliau is a French form of bawdy verse, and behind "venereal" is Venus: Florida, for Stevens, is rampant, erotic, fecund. These qualities pervade the language itself, so that lyric seems to mimic landscape much as insects mimic flora, and flora mimic insects in turn, in an evolutionary tango that birds as well as mammals are gradually admitted to over the eons. It is an evolution that advances by mirroring. When we perceive the eyes of a peacock's tail, we are spooked by the illusion of being seen; yet behind the "fake" eyes is, inarguably, a supple intelligence that proceeds by imitation and analogy. An inanimate force drives species to specific ends: reproduction and adaptation, or change. Language is the same: it makes more of itself, and it adapts. In "Notes Toward a Supreme Fiction," Stevens formulated it thus: "It Must Change .... It Must Give Pleasure."[19]

No one else makes so explicit the connection between language and fecundity, language and biological ornament. Stevens is a rebuke to the pavophobic reader who equates drabness with directness, directness with truth. "Anecdote of the Prince of Peacocks," from *Harmonium*, begins,

> In the moonlight
> I met Berserk,
> In the moonlight

> On the bushy plain.
> Oh, sharp he was
> As the sleepless.

Who is meeting who here? Is the prince of peacocks speaking, or is Stevens the one meeting the "sun-colored" bird in the oneiric landscape? ("I set my traps/In the midst of dreams.") The two are aspects of one reality—waking and sleeping, sun and moon. Something similar happens in "The Bird with the Coppery, Keen Claws," where a parakeet seems like a stand-in for the peacock:

> Above the forest of the parakeets,
> A parakeet of parakeets prevails,
> A pip of life amid a mort of tails.
>
> (The rudiments of tropics are around,
> Aloe of ivory, pear of rusty rind.)
> His lids are white because his eyes are blind.
>
> He is not paradise of parakeets,
> Of his gold ether, golden alguazil,
> Except because he broods there and is still,
>
> Panache upon panache, his tails deploy
> Upward and outward, in green-vented forms,
> His tip a drop of water full of storms.
>
> But though the turbulent tinges undulate
> As his pure intellect applies its laws,
> He moves not on his coppery, keen claws.
>
> He munches a dry shell while he exerts
> His will, yet never ceases, perfect cock,
> To flare, in the sun-pallor of his rock.

With a counterpointing of *p*'s and *k*'s in its keyword (as much of peacock as of parakeet), the flamboyance of the poem is a match for nature's "golden alguazil" (a Spanish or Portuguese word derived from Arabic, it means "minister," a governor or master of arms on a ship). "Parakeet" itself is a word from the mid-sixteenth century—either Old French *paroquet*, Italian *parrocchetto*, or Spanish *periquito*, and therefore a legacy of the conquistadors. A pip can be a small, hard seed from a fruit or the dot on a domino. The "rudiments of the tropics" include aloes and avocados (once known as the alligator pear—"of rusty rind"). "Panache," as Stevensian a word as they come, is from the French for "feather." The height of style, of course, is raised by the feather in your cap. And by the logic of the visual, the set of feathers must "flare" like flame, like flamboyance. This is style as nature conceives it: mimicry and echo. The poem also mimics the pair of claws perching on its branch—by offering us tercets in which one unrhymed line is followed by the rhyming pair that clinches it.

Such flamboyance can be ungenerously reduced to mere decorativeness. Stevens did battle against this reductiveness, but as the glittering twenties crashed into the precarious thirties, aesthetics became a battleground. Social realism threatened to flatten the possibilities for description and imagination. To his friend Ronald Latimer he wrote in 1935,

> This leaves two questions: Whether I accept the common opinion that my verse is essentially decorative, and whether my landscapes are real or imagined. I have delayed answering your letter because I was on the point of saying that I did not agree with the opinion that my verse is decorative, when I remembered that when *Harmonium* was in the making there was a time when I liked the idea of images and images alone, or images and the music of verse together. I then believed in pure poetry, as it was called.
>
> I still have a distinct liking for that sort of thing. But we live in a different time, and life means a good deal more to us nowadays than literature does.

...I don't at all like the words decorative and formal....here people who speak about the thing at all speak of my verse as aesthetic. But I don't like any labels, because I am not doing one thing all the time.[20]

"The Bird with the Coppery, Keen, Claws" tells us explicitly that the bird's beauty isn't essentially decorative, nor is it mindless: its plumage is precisely where "a pure intellect applies its laws." The poet, too, is fulfilling his mimetic instinct, cued by the prolificity of nature to make abundant language.

*

Florida signifies beauty: iridescence, foliage, perfumed air, and outrageously colorful winged waders. But beauty is just the outward manifestation of an innate tendency to order, "laws." Stevens's definitive poem about the pure intellect and its laws will turn out to be "The Idea of Order at Key West," where a woman singing on the shore as she walks marshals pattern and form out of the noise of formless surf, and a "blessed rage for order" seizes even the lights that demarcate the littoral. He insisted that this was not mere fancy: "I want man's imagination to be completely adequate in the face of reality."[21]

"The Idea of Order at Key West," written in the thirties, has an urgent, austere edge to it, but the poems in *Harmonium*, like "The Bird with the Keen, Coppery Claws," insisted on playfulness, even comedy, as another intrinsically natural principle. We see this in another "early poem of order" from *Harmonium*, "Homunculus et la Belle Etoile," in which the ordering principle is also feminine: it is Venus, figured in the evening star. "About *Homunculus*," wrote Stevens to Latimer, "I had forgotten about the ultimate Plato and the torments of confusion. That, after all, is what that poem is about."[22]

> In the sea, Biscayne, there prinks
> The young emerald, evening star,

> Good light for drunkards, poets, widows,
> And ladies soon to be married.

The light of Venus "conducts," writes the poet, the otherwise haphazard thoughts of four categories of distracted people, as well as the "movements of fishes." Meanwhile, as Venus harmonizes and composes the chaotic movements of these creatures, it calms excogitated philosophers, who succumb at last to "charm":

> It might well be that their mistress
> Is no gaunt fugitive phantom.
> She might, after all, be a wanton,
> Abundantly beautiful, eager,
>
> Fecund,
> From whose being by starlight, on sea-coast,
> The innermost good of their seeking
> Might come in the simplest of speech.

The rhyme—or, rather, transfiguration—of "phantom" into "wanton" is key to the poem: to be wanton is to be playful. Thus, the light of Venus "prinks" ("late sixteenth century: probably related to archaic *prank* 'dress or adorn in a showy manner'").[23] And yet it seems that the ultimate outcome of this prinking is that the philosopher is finally reduced to "the simplest of speech." It is a typical Stevensian perambulation to suggest that "elaboration" (note the word "labor" imbedded there) is required to arrive at the essential. And by merry coincidence, "prink" came into our language around the time that the slang word for brothel was "Academy."

This playful poem—a playful poem about the significance of play in the composition of order—serves as a preface to Stevens's chef-d'oeuvre, "The Comedian as the Letter C," which sequentially follows "Homunculus et la Belle Etoile" in *Harmonium*. Here, rich vocabulary and playful buoyancy culminate in a long, ambitious poem that allegorizes a sea journey. The hero, Stevens's alter ego (with hints of Judge Powell), is Crispin, whose name hearkens back to Ben Jonson's chastened poetaster Crispinus. Its first line, and the premise from which the whole poem unfolds, is "Nota: man is the intelligence of his soil," which grounds utterance—including poetry—in geography, geology, and climate. If interactions between soil and weather determine what can be grown and consumed in any place, by extension they determine the language that emerges from the man who eats there. A poet is just another species of fruition.

The plot is simple. Crispin is a man leaving his native soil on a ship journey. He is kin to explorers and buccaneers, having

> an eye most apt in gelatines and jupes,
> Berries of villages, a barber's eye,
> An eye of land, of simple salad-beds,
> Of honest quilts, the eye of Crispin, hung
> On porpoises instead of apricots.

If related to buccaneers, then also to Shakespeare, whose *Tempest* was possibly inspired by descriptions of the Bermudas, and whose most fanciful speeches across his oeuvre—uttered by Caliban, Mercutio, Titania, Enobarbus—are composed of inventive lists like marvelous bills of lading.

So here we are in a world of swashbuckling ornamentation. "Crispin,/The lutanist of fleas, the knave, the thane,/The ribboned stick, the bellowing breeches, cloak/Of China, cap of Spain...And general lexicographer of mute/And maidenly greenhorns" (in contrast to, say, Thomas Nashe's "inkhorne changelings").

"Could Crispin stem verboseness in the sea?" Stevens asks. "Bordeaux to Yucatan, Havana next,/And then to Carolina." This ship voyage, then, is supposed to remake Crispin as a man in confrontation with reality, the *thing itself*, and put to rest his doting over words and other imaginary paradises.

Yet, "in Yucatan, the Maya sonneteers/Of the Caribbean amphitheatre,/In spite of hawk and falcon, green toucan/And jay, still to the night-bird made their plea." Crispin is not out of the verbal woods yet:

> The fabulous and its intrinsic verse
> Came like two spirits parleying, adorned
> In radiance from the Atlantic coign,
> For Crispin and his quill to catechize.

If the Yucatan is poetry in its essential tropical gaudiness, the Carolinas teach Crispin the sensuality of decay:

> A river bore
> The vessel inward. Tilting up his nose,
> He inhaled the rancid rosin, burly smells
> Of dampened lumber, emanations blown
> From warehouse doors, the gustiness of ropes,
> Decays of sacks, and all the arrant stinks
> That helped him round his rude aesthetic out.
> He savored rankness like a sensualist.
> He marked the marshy ground around the dock,
> The crawling railroad spur, the rotten fence,
> Curriculum for the marvellous sophomore.

The aesthete as "sophomore" discovers "prose," that is, a prosaism that can also be transformed into the stuff of poetry. Now Crispin is able to revise his initial thesis to "Note: his soil is man's intelligence./That's better. That's worth crossing seas to find." It seems to me that Stevens is allegorizing two dilemmas faced by many poets: how to continually refresh the senses so that new perceptions feed new poems and how to allow "reality" into the poem without diminishing either reality or the poem. It's hard to do from inside the prose of one's daily life. Stevens's journeys to Florida served this very purpose: only by immersion in the real could he escape the phantoms of imagination that only repeat themselves. "Here was prose"—reality—"More exquisite than any tumbling verse."

Then Crispin plans a colony:

> The man in Georgia waking among pines
> Should be pine-spokesman. The responsive man,
> Planting his pristine cores in Florida,
> Should prick thereof, not on the psaltery,
> But on the banjo's categorical gut,
> Tuck tuck, while the flamingos flapped his bays.

The idea doesn't last long; Crispin turns hermit, "confined." But also "cosseted, condoned." The soil is "suzerain." The continent is "matinal."

> The words of things entangle and confuse.
> The plum survives its poems.

The nutritious plum survives a fusillade of bejeweled words. It survives *cossetted, suzerain, carouse, fiscs*. It survives *matinal, obliquities, harlequined,* and *mauved*. It survives "fugal requiems," where "fugue" is kin to *centrifugal* and *fugitive* and *refugee*: the outward bound and displaced. Thus, the loan words, displaced words, that resound from the Latin (*personae, mulctings*), French (*demoiselle, capuchins*), Italian (*pronunciamento, buffo*), Arabic (*azure*), and Sanskrit (*palankeen*).

Hence, "effective colonizer."

"The Comedian as the Letter C," with its vigorous assertion of vocabulary (I can't help but continue to list and recite the divine babble: paladin, bellicose, prolegomena, caprice, marimba...), is a restoration of the gallimaufry that Ben Jonson satirized in *Poetaster*. We can even go so far as to say he restores the prestige of creolization to English, which Nashe and others argued so mightily against in the sixteenth century. What Crispin's journey seems to tell us is that our instinct for ornamentation is to be found in the cradle of our species, the cradle of all species, the tropics: that our proliferation of words is simply biological evolution by other means—and even the category of "foreign" language is an artificial barrier to entry.

All this underscores the "comedy" of Crispin: it is not primarily an argument—it is high verbal slapstick. Stevens rejected the notion that his poetry was merely decorative, but it is equally true that in his insistence that the "intelligence" can end up spoiling poetry, he makes a space for the apparently decorative and the apparently silly to challenge intellectual rigidity and aridity. The decorative is, after all, a naked appeal to the senses and therefore physical pleasure and comfort. The very title of Crispin's poem pokes fun at seriousness and offers the materiality of a single—but endlessly variable, as we shall see—letter of the alphabet as a sensual musical element, a silly decoration, and proliferative principle. Stevens's letters make it clear enough: "Looked up cassoulet," he wrote to Henry Church. "There is no such word, notwithstanding the menu card at Chambord. Yet how much it seems that there ought to be. To be Cartesian about it: the thing was a true haricot."[24]

And to his benefactor, the small press publisher Ronald Lane Latimer, in 1935:

> By the letter C I meant the sound of the letter C; what was in my mind was to play on that sound throughout the poem. While the sound of that letter has more or less variety, and includes, for instance, K and S, all its shades may be said to have a comic aspect. Consequently, the letter C is a comedian. But if I had made that perfectly clear, susceptible readers might have read the poem with ears like elephants' [sic] listening for the play of this sound as people at a concert listen for the sounds indicating Till Eulenspeigel in Strauss' music....As a rule, people very much prefer to take the solemn views of poetry.[25]

And to another patron, Hy Simons, in 1940:

> You know the old story about St. Francis wearing bells around his ankles so that, as he went about his business, the crickets and so on would get out of his way and not be tramped on. Now, as Crispin moves through the poem, the sounds of the letter C accompany him, as the sounds of the crickets, etc. must have accompanied St. Francis. I don't mean to say that there is an incessant din, but you ought not to be able to read very far in the poem without recognizing what I mean. The sounds of the letter C include all related or derivative sounds. For instance, X, TS and Z. To illustrate: In "Bubbling felicity in Cantilene" the soft C with the change to the hard C, once you notice it, ought to make that line a little different from what it was before. Sometimes the sounds speak all over the place, as, for example, in the line "Exchequering from piebald fiscs unkeyed" The word exchequering is about as full of the sounds of C as any word that I can think of. You have to think of this incidentally as you read the poem; you cannot think of it directly.... You have to read the poem and hear all this whistling and mocking and stressing and, in a minor way, orchestrating, going on in the background, or to say it as a lawyer might say it, "in, on or about the words."[26]

Stevens creates a raucous cacophony (from the Greek, "ill-sounding") as a tropical background full of squawking macaws and frogs, crickets and cicadas. That's what Florida sounds like. Copernicus, Columbus, colonization. Connoisseur, creole, concupiscence, ice cream. Clavicle, key, chord. Comedy, creation.

A final c-word: common. Stevens wanted to be common: "I wanted to get to the center...I wanted to share the common life....People say that I live in a world of my own: that sort of thing."[27] This vision of commonality is ethical and comical, as in Shakespeare: one sees Trinculo and Stephano and Caliban in "a photograph of a lot of fat men and women in the woods, drinking beer and singing Hi-li Hi-lo." (One hears Powell and his buddies in this, too.) Something of this spirit pervades a short prose piece, "Cattle Kings of Florida," about the historic herding of cattle down the peninsula to Punta Rassa, near Fort Myers, which "saw thousands of Florida's free range cattle rafted out to Spanish ships bound for Havana and in turn saw thousands of Spain's golden coins turned over to the cattle barons who lived on scattered and unfenced ranches in the interior."[28] There wasn't any society below St. Augustine then. The Cuban cattle trade boom came to a gradual end after the Spanish–American War, and men on the make turned their sights to other profit centers. But Stevens treasures this wild pioneering moment of men herding cattle through the lightning, over the swamps, making fortunes, setting up the first free schools, or donating parkland. Independent men, living by their wits, with gentleman's agreements not to steal each other's gold: honor and valor. Then real estate takes over.

And tourism. In 1926, Stevens wrote to his editor at *Poetry* magazine, Harriet Monroe: he had accompanied his cohort on a trip of several weeks on a boat from Miami to Key West, "up the Gulf to Thousand Islands...then by way of Cape Sable to Long Key and back to Miami." He complained about Miami: "Miami which used to seem isolated and a place for exotic hermits is now a jamboree of hoodlums."[29] Already the mobs are swelling, an inflection point occurring. In 1935, even Key West will have succumbed: "We may move elsewhere for Key West is no longer quite the delightful affectation it once was. Who wants to share green cocoanut ice cream with these strange monsters who snooze in the porches of this once forlorn hotel."[30]

By 1940, Stevens had fallen out of love with Florida. For one thing, he could no longer nurture the fantasy of being an Adam or a Crusoe: "Key West, unfortunately, is becoming rather literary and artistic."[31] The man who insisted on the metaphysical precept "it must change" did not, in the end, wish Florida to change. To Samuel French Morse he wrote in 1943,

> Although Miami Beach is now a bit like the land of Oz, it was once an isolated spot by the sea, where it was as easy to enjoy mere "being" as it was to breathe the air. And what it was once is still to be found all over Florida.... My particular Florida shrinks from anything like Miami Beach. In any case, unless your mind is made up, you may find that you have picked up an individual Florida of your own which will keep coming back to you long after you are back home. I used to find the place violently affective.[32]

His 1936 volume, *Ideas of Order*, opens with "Farewell to Florida," a premonition of his final break: "Go on, high ship, since now, upon the shore/The snake has left its skin upon the floor."[33] It sets up a dichotomy between "her mind"—that is, Florida's, nature's—and the mind of men in the north toward which his ship is bound. His imagery, unified by a metonymic graveyard, looks forward to Bishop's bone imagery of the keys: first "Key West sank downward under massive clouds," then

>   The palms were hot
> As if I lived in ashen ground, as if
> The leaves in which the wind kept up its sound
> From my North of cold whistled in a sepulchral South....
> How content I shall be in the North to which I sail
> And to feel sure and to forget the bleaching sand.[34]

"I loved her once."[35] Maybe it was significant that, after eighteen years of promises, he finally brought his wife and daughter with him on his valedictory trip to the Keys. He could take leave of the mistress of his imagination once Elsie arrived to dispel its magic.

At any rate, he was older, and "violently affective" feelings were in the past. His geographical imagination shifted northward to Pennsylvania, the terrain of his birth, and—very un-Crusoe-like—he developed an interest in genealogy, pursuing his line of stalwart Dutch ancestors.

3

Marianne Moore

Piracy and Unicorn Horns

I said that no one else makes so explicit the connection between language and fecundity, language and biological ornament, as Stevens. But Marianne Moore, his friend in the art, comes closest in her marriage of zoological knowledge with a linguistic *wunderkammer*. She visited Florida once as an adolescent and found it less appealing than the New England coast, but it was an inspiration behind "Sea Unicorns and Land Unicorns," her great poem of the imagination and a fitting companion poem to "The Comedian as the Letter C."

Born in Kirkwood, Missouri, in 1887, Moore, like Stevens, spent much of her youth in southeastern Pennsylvania. After attending Bryn Mawr College, she and her mother moved to New York. Ill health and penury limited their travel, but Moore, who wrote literary criticism and edited the avant-garde magazine *The Dial* in its heyday, achieved a great deal of renown in her lifetime—a literary celebrity in tricorne hat and cape, writing a victory ode for the Brooklyn Dodgers, on television as a guest on *Today*, a guest on the *Tonight Show*, and paired with Mickey Spillane in a commercial for Braniff Airways.

"Sea Unicorns and Land Unicorns" is the concluding poem of Moore's debut collection, *Observations* (1924). Animals—how we represent them, and how they represent us—are a major motif of the book. The collection launches with an address to a rat and proceeds to investigate a chameleon, a seagull, a rooster, a fish, a snail, a whale, apes, snakes, mongooses, octopuses—and, somewhere in there, a peacock, for good measure. What we share, as well as where we differ, lies in traits: traits strike our eye first, then strike our intuition as behaviors, and personalities and tendencies emerge. The same could be said of poems. In an interview with Donald Hall in *Paris Review*, Moore remarked: "Do the poet and scientist not work analogously? Both are willing to waste effort. To be hard on himself is one of the main strengths of each. Each is attentive to clues, each must narrow the choice, must strive for precision."[1] And yet, she implies in "Sea Unicorns and Land Unicorns," poems are maybe more like chimeras than like wildlife: unicorns rather than peacocks.

Marianne Moore and Wallace Stevens are considered late bloomers, issuing their first books at the ages of thirty-seven (in 1924) and forty-four (in 1923), respectively. In the decade before their debuts—between the heyday of Modernism and the first world war—both published regularly in the avant-garde journal *Others*. It is clear that Moore paid special attention to Stevens's work from early on, because he was mentioned in her first published essay in 1916, "The Accented Syllable," an exploration of sound and sense—their conjunctions and disjunctions—in free verse. She quoted Stevens's sound play approvingly. But she retained doubts about his aestheticism and the direction of *Others* in general as the organ of a postdecadent movement, modeled as it was after Aubrey Beardsley's *The Yellow Book*. Moore could not be a pure aesthete; something in her Presbyterian upbringing militated against pleasure for its own sake, and Stevens veered dangerously toward the amoral or solipsistic. As Moore instructs in "To the Peacock of France," "You were the jewelry of sense;/Of sense, not license."

She was therefore chagrined when she was accused of the same thing by Stevens's champion at *Poetry*, Harriet Monroe. Monroe organized a print symposium in response to Moore's first pamphlet, *Poems*, in 1921. Moore had resisted collecting her work for so long that H.D. colluded with her fellows to publish it behind

Moore's back. Moore was furious at the deception and so all the more agonized when the criticism came:

> This volume is the study of a Marco Polo detained at home. It is the fretting of a wish against wish until the self is drawn, not into a world of air and adventure, but into a narrower self, patient, dutiful and precise. "Those Various Scalpels" is sharper than a diamond. It is as brilliant a poem as any written of late years, and yet it is but a play with the outside of substances and the inside of thoughts too tired to feel emotion. And "Dock Rats" again, or "England," are wrought as finely as the old Egyptians wrought figures from an inch-high piece of emerald; but they lack the one experience of life for which life was created.
>
> The temperament behind the words is not a passive one, however much environment may have forced meditation upon it as a form of "protective coloration." The spirit is robust, that of a man with facts and countries to discover and not that of a woman sewing at tapestries. But something has come between the free spirit and its desire—a psychological uneasiness that is expressed in these few perfect but static studies of a highly evolved intellect.[2]

It's noteworthy that Monroe borrows from the history of exploration—"a Marco Polo detained at home"—and biology—"protective coloration"—to critique Moore. Just as noteworthy is that in the same symposium, Yvor Winters praised Moore extravagantly, yoking her name to Wallace Stevens's and declaring them to be the two greatest poets writing.

Despite her doubts about his moral intentions, Moore was deeply drawn to the tropical gaudiness of Stevens's verse. When, in 1921, Monroe published a set of twelve poems that would soon appear in *Harmonium*, Moore copied out the lines of his "Hibiscus on the Sleeping Shores" in her reading journal:

> Then it was that that monstered moth
> Which had lain folded against the blue
> And the colored purple of the lazy sea,
>
> And which had drowsed along the bony shores,
> Shut to the blather that the water made,
> Rose up besprent and sought the flaming red
>
> Dabbled with yellow pollen—red as red
> As the flag above the old cafe—
> And roamed there all the stupid afternoon.

Clearly the "monstered moth" of Stevens will find its way into the monsters of "Sea Unicorns and Land Unicorns." It's a short leap from moths to monsters, or peacocks to unicorns, or purely aesthetic poems to poems of moral intention.

Stevens and Moore's artistic kinship, based on shared poetic traits, did not lead to a close friendship immediately, but they did write about each other's work with great warmth in public and in private. In 1935, Stevens wrote to an editor: "Miss Moore is not only a complete disintegrator; she is an equally complete reintegrator.... It seems to me that Miss Moore is endeavoring to create a new romantic; that the way she breaks up older forms is merely an attempt to free herself for the pursuit of the thing in which she is interested; and that the thing in which she is interested in all the strange collocations of her work is that which is essential in poetry, always: the romantic. But a fresh romantic."[3] There's that word "collocation," from the Latin "to place together," a word right out of Crispin's treasure chest. The "romantic" was much on his mind in these low days of 1935. Just a few days earlier, he had written to his friend, Ronald Latimer, "When people speak of the romantic, they do so in what the French commonly call a pejorative sense. But poetry is essentially romantic, only the romantic of poetry must be something constantly new.... What one is always doing is keeping the romantic pure: eliminating from it what people speak of as the romantic."[4]

When Stevens wrote a public appreciation of Moore, "A Poet That Matters," he quoted her description of a peacock:

In "The Steeple-Jack" she writes of

> a sea the purple of the peacock's neck is
> paled to greenish azure as Durer changed
> the pine green of the Tyrol to peacock blue.

The strong sounds of *the purple of the peacock's neck* contrast and intermingle with the lighter sounds of *paled to greenish azure* and return again to the strong sounds of the last line.[5]

And likewise, Moore in "On Wallace Stevens" alludes to Stevens's peacocks: "Pictorially, we have in Wallace Stevens an opulence of jungle beauty, arctic beauty, marine beauty, hothouse beauty; and natural beauty. His 'Domination of Black' depicts hemlocks 'in which the sun can only fumble,' that have the majesty of peacocks. He admired the blue-green of pines, could be called 'the spokesman for pines,' his own phrase. He brings alive 'the green vine angering for life, meet for the eye of the young alligator.'"[6]

*

I have descended to the cellar of the University of Florida's Library West, wearing a mask although there is no one around—it is a Sunday during the intermission between the spring semester and summer classes, and the campus is all but deserted, as it was in the first months of the pandemic only a year ago. The book I want is buried in the farthest reaches of the stacks. And then, in the dimness, I discover the stacks won't move. The electronics are on the fritz. So I go down the last row, reaching through the faced-out shelves to pick out books at random from the faced-in shelves, and by following the call numbers I'm able to pinpoint the area where DA 356.W7 should be. I have to draw a chair and climb to the top, but I've successfully plucked it from the blind, immovable stack: *Queen Elizabeth's Maids of Honour* by Violet Wilson. This is the Victorian era account of the Tudor court, which Moore drew on for "Sea Unicorns and Land Unicorns."

From the opening pages, the splendor of Tudor pageantry is portrayed in terms of ornament and learning, learning *as* ornament. "It was an age pre-eminent of romance, a world electric with portents of fresh discoveries; new lands were being sought for, new ventures undertaken, new inventions perfected, new luxuries coming into general use."[7] This salvo could be compared with Moore and Stevens's era: an era of enormous technological change and "new luxuries," but certainly not a romantic era in the wake of a disillusioning world war. The atheistic disenchantment of Modernism, captured in T. S. Eliot's "The Waste Land," moved in counterpoint to its revolutions and innovations. One interpretation of Moore's interest in Wilson's book could be that Stevens was right: they both perceived a need to re-invest the modern world with new romanticism.

Within Wilson's story of Queen Elizabeth's ladies in waiting there is a story about their men, often absent on missions of war or diplomacy or plunder. This provides the slender thread binding Stevens's mythically colonialist voyage, "The Comedian as the Letter C," to "Sea Unicorns and Land Unicorns" via the queen's buccaneers, like Sir John Hawkins:

> and Sir John Hawkins' Florida
> "abounding in land unicorns and lions,
> since where the one is,
> its arch enemy cannot be missing."

John Hawkins was instrumental in the queen's navy; his innovations helped defeat the Spanish Armada, and his privateering in and around Florida and the Caribbean included slave trading and collecting wonders to present to the court. His tall tale regarding Florida is useful for Moore's purposes. His monsters help set up the poem's symbolic counterpoint: lions and unicorns; land and sea; plunderous male explorers and chaste female monarchs; and, most important, the imagination and reality. In the Elizabethan imagination, Florida was a place of great untapped wealth, symbolized by its lush landscape (natural resources being a synecdoche of wealth as well as a material source for it). The Bodleian library contains an anonymous ballad written around 1564 that asks, "Have you not hard of floryda?"

> Have you not hard of floryda,
> A coontre far bewest,
> Where savage pepell planted are
> By nature and by hest,
> Who in the mold
> Fynd glysterynge gold
> and yt for tryfels sell?
> with hy!
> Ye all alonge the watere side,
> Where yt doth eb and flowe,
> Are turkeyse founde and where also
> Do perles in oysteres growe,
> And on the land
> Do cedars stand
> Whose bewty do[th] excel.
> with hy!
> trysky, trym, go trysky, wun not a wallet do well?

Hawkins provides his own account of natural riches from his travelogue:

> The Floridians have pieces of unicornes hornes which they weare about their necks, whereof the Frenchmen obtained

many pieces. Of those unicornes they have many; for that they doe affirme it to be a beast with one horne, which comming to the river to drinke, putteth the same into the water before he drinketh.... Of beasts in this countrey besides deere, foxes, hares, polcats, conies, ownces and leopards, I am not able certeinly to say: but it is thought that there are lions and tygres as well as unicorns; lions especially;... crocodiles, whereof there is great abundance, adders of great bigness..."[8]

This litany is in stark contrast to settlers' fortunes, however. Hawkins in 1565 found French colonists on the St. John's River in "great distress," subsisting on acorns, fitfully mutinying, skirmishing with nearby tribes. In the course of his intrigue with the captain at Fort Caroline, he saved the colony, which was on the verge of being abandoned.

René de Laudonnière, leader of the colony at Fort Caroline, wrote his own account of Hawkins's visit, "L'Histoire notable de la Floride," published in Paris. Hawkins donated salt, wax for candles, vinegar and oil, flour, and rice in exchange for cannon and powder. Laudonnière questioned Hawkins's motives; he refused his offer to transport them back to France, suspecting that Hawkins would then capture the fort for Queen Elizabeth. Hearing of this refusal, the French soldiers mutinied; Laudonnière appeased them by buying Hawkins's sumptuous provisions.

But in saving the colony, Hawkins had only preserved it for a more thorough destruction when the Spanish, a few miles to the south in St. Augustine, decided to drive out the Protestant French once and for all. They seized Fort Caroline, and just as French reinforcements were about to launch an attack on the Spanish in response, a hurricane intervened and wrecked their ships. The Spanish, having gotten wind of those shipwrecked, rode in and massacred most of the survivors—only Catholics and a few useful laborers (and musicians!) were spared. Hence Matanzas ("murdered") Beach, that lovely and popular spit of land between the Atlantic and intracoastal waterway. Had a general circumstance of scarcity, hunger, and embattlement not prevailed, the shipwreck survivors might have been spared. As it was, leaders had sailed off for supplies, present supplies were dwindling away, and hostilities with native tribes threatened.

*

Something in splendor itself is understood to be cruel. Why is it that, in *The Scarlet Letter*, Hester Prynne's badge of shame, embroidered with gold thread, is at once splendid and sinister? It is almost alive in its scintillations, in its ability to transmit heat to whoever touches it. Nathaniel Hawthorne keeps reminding us that there is a sumptuary insult in her handiwork, an insult to the somber hues of the Puritan settlement. But what I recall most vividly is that the captain of the Spanish ship that Hester believes is her salvation—that will bear her and her lover and child back to Bristol—is decked out in buccaneer splendor: ribbons, gold lace, gold chains, and feathers. He has a "galliard air" incongruous with the settlers, but permitted to a figure of transit.

While Elizabeth's courtiers went to sea to wrest the title of the greatest empire of the world from the Spanish, King Philip II faced unrest at home. Rumors that a teenage girl, Lucrecia de León, daughter of a solicitor, was dreaming prophesies that were coming true reached the ears of two theologians at court, Alonso de Mendoza and Lucas de Allende. They took her under their wing and put her to work: that is, to sleep. They started transcribing hundreds of dreams, which predicted, among other things, that the Armada would be defeated. Lucrecia's prophecies cried out for political reform. Such visions were taken to be directly inspired by God, though women's visions were allegedly prey to "diabolical" influences. The young girl's dreams were themselves weaponized by the courtiers, who found her a useful mouthpiece.

Over four hundred dreams are recorded in the annals of the Inquisition, which arrested and tried Lucrecia and her spiritual advisors for blasphemy and sedition over a period of five years, beginning in 1590, when she was twenty-one. The command to arrest her came from the very top. After the defeat of the Armada and Francis Drake's incendiary raid on Cádiz—dubbed "the singeing of the King of Spain's beard" by Drake himself—Philip felt himself under threat both at home and abroad. The streets of Madrid were overrun with street preachers predicting apocalyptic scenarios, but Lucrecia—middle class, with a good reputation, and reported to be quite beautiful—had influence.

In one dream, an artichoke at the head of the king's bed was plucked of all its leaves by the royal tax collectors as the monarch slept. In another dream, a cart pulled by bulls bore a tower beside a dead lion, with a dead eagle atop it, its breast split open. The cart's wheels were stained with blood and as it moved over the land it ran people over; others were chained to the cart and proclaiming that the world was ending.[9]

Shortly before she was arrested, Lucrecia dreamed of a barebreasted Amazon riding a bull through Madrid. The Amazon's arms were covered with snakes and she decapitated children as she rode. In another dream, Lucrecia saw her again, holding a lantern, with a black bear on a leash. Words were written in blood on her back: "I am the suffering of Spain and I come as a woman to show you the little strength you have to defend yourselves."[10]

In 1587, Lucrecia visited London in a dream. There, she saw a middle-aged woman called the queen with a dead lamb in her lap, its stomach cut open, and her hands scooping its insides. When she commanded a bystander to drink the blood and the woman refused, the queen wrathfully drew her sword and cut off the woman's head. This would seem to refer to the execution of Mary Stuart, Queen of Scots, in February of that year.[11]

In another dream about Elizabeth, in 1589, Lucrecia saw the queen gloating over the silver her men had captured from the Spanish fleet.[12]

*

Yet it was Lucrecia's lack of schooling and near illiteracy that argued in favor of her innocence, and of the veracity of her visions. In *Lucrecia's Dreams: Politics and Prophecy in Sixteenth-Century Spain*, Richard L. Kagan notes, "The transcribed versions of Lucrecia's dreams are written in what Mendoza referred to as 'estilo llano,' a plain or unadorned style, a phrase intended to distinguish the colloquial language of Lucrecia's dictations from the consciously artistic, highly mannered style of courtly or literary Castilian. Lucrecia's dreams are related in a conversational tone, and even in dialogue with King Philip, she uses the familiar *tú*."[13] Style, then, is called to account in a court of law. A sumptuous style denotes aristocracy, but also frivolity and waste. If Mendoza did mastermind Lucrecia's dreams, the motive lay in his criticism of the monarch's extravagance. He despised the Escorial, "the royal monastery whose construction took fourteen years and cost nearly five million ducats, a sum roughly equivalent to one year's treasury receipts from the Indies, or almost as much as Philip expended on the Armada." It was "built at the cost of the poor." "God can be served...with fewer high walls and haughty towers, slate roofs, brocades, gold, silver, precious stones, pearls, and extraordinary marbles."[14]

Mendoza thought the beasts in the royal forests were better treated than the average Spaniard: "This king wants to be a king of animals rather than men, because he gives more to those beasts than to his vassals, since he does not kill the former for erecting fences and barriers and if anyone kills his deer they are whipped. On the other hand, after the church gave him 600,000 ducats for one hundred galleys to defend the coasts, he did not want to do it until the enemies came to seize captives and to rob the land, as in Cádiz and elsewhere."[15]

Mendoza was sentenced to seclusion in a monastery, where he died surrounded by his books and artworks. Lucrecia, who bore a daughter in prison, was convicted but allowed to go free. She and her child disappeared from the public record; she did not go back to her father's house, she did not join her lover, and her name does not appear on the official register of beggars. Everything about her vanished into history, except the record of her extraordinary protest: her dreams and her "estilo llano."

*

Splendor in Moore, as in Stevens, is bound up with ornament. Pirating text from Violet Wilson's *Queen Elizabeth's Maids of Honour*, Moore connects "embroideries" with fabulous fictive creatures. "Embroidery" has long been a metaphor for storytelling, and even verbal deception. Wilson suggests that the emphasis on learning and language at court was of a piece with the love of finery: "Elizabeth appointed a librarian at Whitehall Palace, and under his charge the shelves quickly filled with books of the time.... These were especially bound in coloured velvet, stamped in gold with the Queen's Arms, and the clasps encrusted with precious stones. Foreign literature, also, was well represented, the Queen being an exceptionally clever linguist. She not only read but spoke various tongues with fluent accuracy, could address the universities in Greek, trounce a malapert ambassador in vigorous Latin, or fish for compliments with equal facility in French, Italian, or Spanish."[16] Like Crispin the exotic lexicographer, "Young men who traveled on the Continent brought back foreign words, and clothes in general use in the countries they had visited."[17] Compare the description of the books, and variegated language, with the finery worn at court. "Seated on a pile of gold-covered cushions Elizabeth passed her wardrobe in review, as one by one Mary Scudamore and her helpers brought forward dresses for inspection. Many and of infinite variety were they":

> A forepart of white satten, embrodered all over with pansies, little roses, knotts, and a border of mulberries, pillars and pomegranets, of Venice golde, sylver, and sylke of sondrye colours.
>
> One forepart of green satten, embrodered all over with sylver, like beasts, fowles, and fishes.

> A petticoat, embrodered all over slightly with snakes of Venice gold and silver and some O's, with a faire border embrodered like seas, cloudes, and rainbowes.
>
> One forepart of white satten, embrodered all over with spiders, flies, and roundells, with cobwebs, of Venice golde and tawny silk.[18]

This is the description that Moore borrows (or, in keeping with the spirit of the explorers, pirates) for "Sea Unicorns and Land Unicorns" in two places in the poem. For Moore, the artifice of the dresses has a magical purpose, mapping the land and its riches in flora and fauna onto the monarch's person. Likewise, the poem's artifice has a magical purpose. Full of richly described objects—maps, embroidered screens, dresses, a sky chart—it is itself elaborately (that is, with labor) embroidered. It is also a collage, inflected with many diverse quotations, not only from Wilson but also from Henry James and J. A. Symonds, Herodotus and Pliny, travelogues and magazines. With its dizzyingly rapid cuts—or darts and seams—this poem presents itself to us as a chimerical construction: part original language, part borrowed language; part poem, part prose. It *is* the unicorn. Thus, Moore becomes the figure of the Virgin at the end, and the unicorn is the poem that cannot be willed, but must be wooed:

> upon the map, "upon her lap,"
> its "mild wild head doth lie."

As Stevens noted, it takes a lot of prinking to arrive at the "simplest of speech." These rhymes—map/lap, mild/wild—serve as a musical coda, but they also lead us by association to the conceptual rhyme between unicorn and lion, peace and power, poet and queen. "I am governed," Moore told Donald Hall, "by the pull of a sentence as the pull of a fabric is governed by gravity."[19]

In December 2023, I got to see some of these Elizabethan dresses in large-scale paintings assembled at the Metropolitan

Museum of Art for a special exhibition on the Tudors. In the largest surviving portrait of Queen Elizabeth, the Ditchley portrait, she is standing on a map of England, and the heavens behind her are divided between day and night, sunshine and thunderhead. This dress is white, appliqued with flowers and encrusted with gems and pearls. In another portrait, she holds the rainbow in her right hand while her left puff sleeve sports an intricately embroidered, coiled green serpent.

Here, too, is the portrait Moore would have given much thought to: Elizabeth in a dress whose voluminous skirt depicts creatures of land, air, and sea amid exquisite flora.

Like Elizabeth, Marianne Moore was a redhead. She was the most famous flame-haired girl at Bryn Mawr in her time. Alfred Kreymborg described her as "astonishing...with Titian hair...and a mellifluous flow of polysyllables which held every man in awe."[20] Did she, then, feel a special kinship with the virgin queen, based on their coloring, when she wrote of the unicorn coming to lay its head on her lap? And as the eldest child who commanded the pronouns *he* and *him* in her fatherless family, telling her younger brother Warner that she was *his* brother, did she hear the *vir* in *virgin* as its etymology demanded—the Latin for *man*?

This virgin queen never married either; she lived with her mother until the older woman's death, when Marianne was fifty-nine. She moved out of the apartment they shared in Brooklyn—indeed, they had slept in the same bed for most of their years together—and moved to Greenwich Village. Like a much-revered queen, she had the honor of having a replica of her parlor at 35 W. 9th Street installed in the Rosenbach Museum in Philadelphia in 1972, the year she died. I was living about ten miles away at the time, in Northeast Philadelphia. I had just turned three.

*

Something in splendor itself is understood to be cruel. Leaving the exhibit and taking a whirl around the museum, which was nothing if not a palace—I was struck, like a bell, again and again. In a different wing was another large exhibit, of paintings that "trick the eye"—trompe l'oeil—from the Dutch realists to the Cubists. Here were the fruits of illusionism—literally, the grapes of Zeuxis at which the birds were said to peck, the curtain of Parrhasius, which it was said Zeuxis tried to pull aside to get at the painting. But the curtain was the painting. So Zeuxis had to cede the laurel to Parrhasius. Here, too, were tables with knives you wished to grasp to slice the bread, beer you wished to drink out of glasses etched so finely that they were surely gathering the toxic dust of the ages.

And then, in a further room, the furthest thing you could get from naturalistic goblets and cutlery: the annual Christmas tree festooned with Neapolitan angels from the Bourbon dynasty. If the entire Metropolitan Museum was in a way a descendent of Elizabeth I's palace—filled with the treasures her courtiers brought back from their global expeditions—these angels transcended geography. They came from the annals of poetry: the Bible, Caedmon.

*

Just as the explorers brought back natural wonders—"how a voyager obtained the horn of a sea unicorn to give to Queen Elizabeth/who thought it worth a hundred thousand pounds"— Moore, too, is in the business of obtaining rarities to present to her reader; her sources provide a map of her reading, which takes on the aspects of a journey. Violet Wilson again: "Many were the curiosities which the explorers brought home as presents for the ladies. The Queen naturally had first choice, and to her fell the unicorn's horn valued at (pounds) 100,000, which became one of the treasures of Windsor. A sea-unicorn's horn, presented by Martin Frobisher, was handed over to Mrs. Scudamore to hang among Her Majesty's dresses as a preventative of poison."[21] There, then, is the seed of Moore's vision—the horn (most likely from a narwhal) hanging among the queen's dresses gets transposed in her imagination to the "mild wild head" in the lap of the virgin. "Curiosities" points back to the phenomenon of the mind and the repository of the intelligence: mild, wild, and dangerous to know.

Wilson recounts other legends of animal and chimeras that implicitly inform Moore's poem: not only do unicorns and lions exist in antipathy, but also mirrors were important to arrest tigers in their tracks; a basilisk seeing his own reflection would immediately expire. Crocodiles cried to lure sympathetic prey closer; pelicans could bring their dead offspring back to life by offering their own blood as nourishment, and the phoenix lived for hundreds of years before self-immolating, then rising again from the ashes. Manticores had "the head of a man with three rows of teeth in each jaw, the body of a bear, legs of a lion, tail of a scorpion, and voice of a trumpet."[22] Mermaids and sea serpents lured sailors to their death, as in Sir John Davies's "Orchestra:"

> What meane the Mermayds when they daunce and sing
> But certaine death unto the Marriner?
> What tydings doe the dauncing Dilphins bring
> But that some dangerous storme approcheth nere?
> Then sith both Love and Dauncing lyveries beare
> Of such ill hap, unhappy may I prove,
> If sitting free, I either daunce or love.[23]

Joseph Brodsky was prompted to meditate on chimeras in Venice, whose mascot is a winged lion, and where half-fish half-human creatures ornament the palazzos: "On the whole, all these nightmarish creatures—dragons, gargoyles, basilisks, female-breasted sphinxes, winged lions, Cerberuses, Minotaurs, centaurs, chimeras—that come to us from mythology (which by rights, should have the status of classical surrealism) are our self-portraits, in the sense that they denote the species' genetic memory of evolution. Small wonder that here, in this city sprung from water, they abound."[24] He also shared Moore's intuition that unicorns and lions do need each other, musing on the imagery of St. George slaying the dragon: "In a line of work involving the dipping of a pen into an inkpot, one can identify with both. After all, there is no saint without a monster—not to mention the ink's octopal affinity."[25]

Thus, fantastical as chimeras might seem, they do not differ in kind but in degree from actual descriptions of actual animals:

> "Anchorites do not dwell in theatres," and peacocks do not
> flourish in a cell.
> Why make distinctions? The results were well
> When you were on the boards; nor were your triumphs
> bought
> At horrifying sacrifice of stringency.
> You hated sham; you ranted up
> And down through the conventions of excess;
> Nor did the King love you the less
> Nor did the world,
> In those chief interest and for whose spontaneous
> delight, your broad tail was unfurled.

Nor does a narwhal horn seem less fantastical for not being a unicorn horn. An anecdote of Sir Walter Raleigh introducing tobacco and the sweet potato to Ireland reminds us that the fruits we take for granted now were wonders five hundred years ago. Moore's genius in ending a collection of poems called *Observations*, in which the flora and fauna of the natural world in the wake of Charles Darwin's discoveries culminates in a creature from myth, is a statement about the vision of poetry and the projections of the imagination beyond what is possible to what is *imaginable*. By positing polarities—lions versus unicorns in one poem, anchorites versus peacocks in another, Moore dialectically works out that beauty, properly understood, *is* a visionary moral undertaking.

Resplendent siblings, both Moore and Stevens blended the natural world—the world of perceptions—with a construct of the imagination. As Stevens wrote in a letter, "I have been going to Florida for twenty years, and all of the Florida poems have actual backgrounds. The real world seen by an imaginative man may very well seem like an imaginative construction."[26] Moore explicitly selected Hawkins's story of chimeras, woven into a historical account of the discovery of Florida, as the subject of a collaged poem in which the imaginative creature comes of its own accord to the lap of the virgin. Where Stevens emphasized the venereal and Venusian in Florida, Moore countered with something purer, neither phantom nor wanton. Her Florida is curious, where curios originate, and where curators go to curate.

Coda

"Sea Unicorns and Land Unicorns" wasn't the first poem to originate in a secondhand account of Florida exploration. That honor belongs to "Kubla Khan" by Samuel Taylor Coleridge (written around November 1797), whose lines about underground caverns and rivers and exploding fountains derived from William Bartram's *Travels through North and South Carolina, Georgia, and East Florida*, a version of which was published in London in 1792. Coleridge's notebook from the time contains a line from it— "Some wilderness plot, green & fountainous & unviolated by Man"—that hints at the poem to come, but the classics scholar Caroline Alexander, who researched the Florida–Coleridge connection in her book *The Way to Xanadu* (1993), believes that key passages in Bartram's *Travels* provide exact coordinates for the poem's geography: "From Bartram's itinerary we know that the little Isle of Palms and mighty fountain were to be found in the same corner of the Florida landscape: the mighty fountain is both Manatee Springs, some twenty miles west of Gainesville, and Salt

Springs, set squarely in the Ocala National Forest; the Isle of Palms lies off Rocky Point on the northwest shore of Lake George and the meandering sacred river is Salt Springs Run, which winds five miles from the springs down to the great sea of Lake George."[27] Nor was Coleridge the only writer on whom Bartram made a deep impression: "The *Travels* was a singular inspiration for the Romantics, and its images were insinuated, in lesser degrees, into the works of Wordsworth, Southey, Shelley, Thomas Campbell, Tennyson and Emerson."[28]

William Bartram's expedition through the American South was sponsored by King George of England more than a hundred years after John Hawkins reported to Queen Elizabeth. He was in the area of Gainesville around the summer of 1774. His account of the landscape, like so many, swells to an ode to cornucopia:

> The pompous Palms of Florida, and glorious Magnolia, strikes us with the sense of dignity and magnificence; the expansive umbrageous Live-Oak with awful veneration, the Carica papaya, supercilious with all the harmony of beauty and gracefulness; the Lillium superbum represents pride and vanity; Kalmia latifolia and Azalea coccinea, exhibit a perfect show of mirth and gaiety; the Illicium Floridanum, Crinum Floridanum, Convallaria majalis of the Cherokees, and Calycanthus floridus, charm with their beauty and fragrance. Yet they are not to be compared for usefulness with the nutritious Triticum, Zea, Oryza, Solanum tuberosum, Musa, Convolvulus, Batata, Rapa, Orchis, Vitis vinifera, Pyrus, Olea; for clothing with Linum Cannabis, Gossypium, Morus; for medical virtues, Hyssopus, Thymus, Anthemis nobilis, Papaver somniferum, Quinquina, Rheum rhabarbarum, Pisum, &c.[29]

In his description of the Florida aquifer and lakes southeast of Gainesville, we hear the language that Coleridge would transfigure into poetry. Here is Bartram: "Just under my feet, was the inchanting and amazing crystal fountain, which incessantly threw up, from dark, rocky caverns below, tons of water every minute, forming a basin...which meanders six miles through green meadows, pouring its limpid waters into the great Lake George, where they seem to remain pure and unmixed."[30] And here is Coleridge:

> And from this chasm, with ceaseless turmoil seething,
> As if this earth in fast thick pants were breathing,
> A mighty fountain momently was forced:
> Amid whose swift half-intermitted burst
> Huge fragments vaulted like rebounding hail,
> Or chaffy grain beneath the thresher's flail:
> And mid these dancing rocks at once and ever
> It flung up momently the sacred river.
> Five miles meandering with a mazy motion
> Through wood and dale the sacred river ran,
> Then reached the caverns measureless to man,
> And sank in tumult to a lifeless ocean.[31]

The twentieth-century British poet laureate, Ted Hughes, was also struck by Coleridge's interest in Bartram's description of alligator mating calls, speculating that it lay behind the descriptions of "woman wailing for her demon lover" and "as if this earth in fast thick pants were breathing."[32]

Recently, I walked to the Sweetwater Overlook on the Hawthorne bike trail in Gainesville, and I stared for a long time at Payne's Prairie, which at this time in spring is woven with all shades of juicy green. The Alachua sink is shaped like a basin, emptied of the lake that used to be there. Streams rise and fall still, visible to the eye that day as a long skein of duckweed that an egret followed, scanning for tidbits. Herons, cormorants, anhingas, limpkins, ibises, and bitterns stalked the grasses. In the distance, the sun glinted off the traffic on the state road built on the opposite bluff. When guests come to our city, this is where we take them to see alligators. The abundant marsh hares hopping at the verges, the small flocks of ducks sailing the ponds, seem oblivious to them. On a good day, you might see the wild horses or a small herd of bison.

Educational placards tell us that the Alachua sink contains swallowholes that carry rainwater down into the Florida aquifer, a vast underground river flowing beneath and through our limestone floor. It is a wonder to me that I may be living in proximity to Coleridge's source: rural north central Florida seems to have no connection whatsoever to the English literary canon. But that's the point of underground sources: they don't advertise themselves to the naked eye. You have to look for them.

4

Elizabeth Bishop

A Queer Antique Musical Instrument Floating in the Sea

> Very windy all night & cold to-day. The banana tree leaves have been cut, or slashed by the wind to strips—like Elizabethan [sense of] word "slashed sleeves." —Journals

There it stands: 624 White Street, the first of the "three loved houses" made famous in "One Art." Built around 1889, it was purchased by Elizabeth Bishop and her girlfriend Louise Crane in 1938. It is a model of rectangular symmetry, a so-called eyebrow house of wide, white, vertical boards and pine green shutters set back on a porch, with a pale tin roof extended on pillars over the three second-story windows to keep out the merciless sun. Those windows are balanced by two windows below, on either side of a door. (Through the thick, blurred, aged glass of those double-hung windows, you can almost look through Bishop's eyes.) Palm trees and palmettoes in the front yard give an impression of umbrellas and fans creating a breeze, keeping things cool. In the shady backyard that she once described as having "4 banana trees, two avocado trees, two lime trees, a mango tree, a sour sop tree, and a grape arbor," all that remains of that list is one avocado tree and the mango tree, the latter resplendent with fruit. It is mango and star fruit season. Also, the poinciana trees are in full scarlet regalia and the air is heavy with frangipani; the equally fragrant mock orange is just starting to bloom.

White Street marks the boundary of the Old Town at its easternmost edge, as far from the merrymaking of Duval Street and Mallory Square as it is possible to get. Bishop's house stands in comfortable proximity to the historic cemetery, nineteen acres in which as many as one hundred thousand bodies are buried, a whole city in itself, with whitewashed crypts blinding in the sunlight and unearthly in the moonlight. She writes of it in an unpublished draft called "The Street by the Cemetery":

> The people on little verandahs in the moonlight
> are looking at the graveyard
> like passengers on ship-board.

Dating back to 1847, the cemetery is bounded by streets with feminine names: Angela Street and Margaret Street, Frances Street and Olivia Street. Elizabeth Street is a block away in the other direction. When I coast along this grid at night on my rental bike, it's hard not to conflate their names with the angels whose cool marble wings pierce the dark. The air is heavy with floral scent, though the gravestones are necklaced with plastic flowers. Here, too, style reigns.

The insularity of this necropolis—an island within an island—gives it an aura of fable, as if the redundancy could nullify the logic of death.

*

A couple of months before her twenty-seventh birthday, in December 1936, Bishop traveled to the Keewaydin fishing camp in Naples with Crane. In January she wrote to Marianne Moore:

> It is so wild, and what there is of cultivation seems rather dilapidated and about to become wild again. On the way down we took a very slow train from Jacksonville here. All day long it went through swamps and turpentine camps and palm forests

and in a beautiful pink evening it began stopping at several little stations. The stations were all off at a tangent from the main track and it necessitated first going by, then stopping, backing up, stopping, starting again—with many puffs of white smoke, blowings of the whistle, advice from the loiterers around the station—all to throw off one limp bag of mail.[1]

Like her mentor, she had a keen interest in natural history, an attentiveness to the names of animals and plants, their markings, and their habitats:

The purpose of my trip to Fort Myers was to see Ross Allen wrestle with his alligator and give a lecture on, and exhibit of, snakes. I do wish you could have seen it, Miss Moore. I am so sure you would have liked it. He had two tremendous diamond-backed rattlers; they popped balloons with their fangs, and you could see the venom springing out—it was in a floodlight. Then he extracted venom in a cocktail glass set on a little white table. The rattling sounded like a sewing machine. He had some other beautiful snakes, especially one, a long shiny "chicken snake" vertically striped black and yellow. The Harlequin Coral snake is too small to exhibit that way, but I have seen some lovely ones, and some puff adders.... The part of the show devoted to the alligator was memorable chiefly because Mr. Allen wanted to creep up on it (in a big swimming pool) unnoticed, and yet go on with the lecture. So he slid into the water, and went right on talking. It was quite a sight to see his large solemn baby face apparently floating bodiless on the surface of the water, while from it came his imitations of the alligator's calls: the "bellow," the love call, the warning, and the social call.[2]

This latter description would be transformed into the arresting final lines of her renowned poem, "Florida":

> The alligator, who has five distinct calls:
> friendliness, love, mating, war, and a warning—
> whimpers and speaks in the throat
> of the Indian Princess.

Bishop's initial apprehension of Florida's bounty is in the tradition of "Have you not hard of floryda"; Hawkins, Bartram, and Stevens's "venereal soil", his fantasia of the "cattle kings" and frontier anarchy. The two poets never met, but Bishop had all but committed *Harmonium* to memory as a college student, made a careful study of each new collection (*Ideas of Order* came out a year before her first visit), and discussed his work at length, sometimes critically, with Moore. When she heard rumors that Stevens was at Casa Marina in 1940, she joked to her mentor that she went to lunch there "almost provided with opera glasses" but didn't manage a glimpse of the master.[3]

In fact, a close look at "Florida" suggests that it is a rewriting of Stevens's "Nomad Exquisite." Or rather, it is an expansion of his compressed, imagistic vividness, which leaves out so much of the rot and rankness of subtropical biomass. His "immense dew" and "green vine" are clarified, in Bishop's poem, to "brackish water," "held together by mangrove roots." His "big-finned palm" becomes her "palm trees clatter" just as his "green sides/And gold sides of green sides" becomes her "green hummocks" and "damp gold wings." His "flakes of flames," an image of sublimity, comes into focus when set side by side with her buzzards circling "like stirred-up flakes of sediment." His "forms, flames, and flakes of flames," moreover, revert to their origins as real brushfires: "Smoke from woods-fires filters fine blue solvents./On stumps and dead trees the charring is like black velvet." Finally, Stevens's "eye of the young alligator" becomes Bishop's alligator calls. The disconcerting image, of a deep male bellow erupting from the "Indian princess," can fairly be imagined as Stevens's voice erupting from Bishop's own throat. She would also have known another of Stevens's poems, "Two Figures in Dense Violet Night," which fairly commands the reader:

> Be the voice of night and Florida in my ear.
> Use dusky words and dusky images.
> Darken your speech.

Bishop may also have had those lines in mind when she wrote "Seascape," whose "skeletal lighthouse" rejects "the celestial seascape":

> He thinks that hell rages below his iron feet,
> and that is why the shallow water is so warm,
> and he knows that heaven is not like this.
> Heaven is not like flying or swimming,
> but has something to do with blackness and strong glare
> and when it gets dark he will remember something
> strongly worded to say on the subject.

Known for both her nomadism and her exquisiteness—in the etymological sense of "seeking out"—Bishop both springs from a Stevensian aesthetic and serves as a correction.

*

The aesthetic triangle between Bishop, Stevens, and Moore traverses Florida at its base. Bishop's intense identification with some aspects of Stevens's work is balanced by differences threshed via correspondences (in a double sense) with Moore. Like him, she responded instinctively to the wild lushness—so different from the northern landscapes of her childhood in Nova Scotia and Massachusetts—but she also delved, Moore-like, deeper into its details, with a more precise (or *exquisite*), journalistic eye. Unlike either of her precursors, she reveled in its less scenic aspects:

camps, industrial wharves, hurricane detritus. "Smoke, from the turpentine camp, cabin-chimney, sudden fires in the swamps, plays such a large part in the atmosphere & decorativeness of the Florida landscape."[4] Where Stevens had forged his sensibilities in the romantic 1910s and '20s, she came of age in the social realist '30s. This contrast in sensibility tracks with the sobering counter-influence of W. H. Auden: "When I was in college, and all through the thirties and forties, I and all my friends who were interested in poetry, read him constantly. We hurried to see his latest poem or book, and either wrote as much like him as possible, or tried hard not to. His then leftist politics, his ominous landscape, his intimations of betrayed loves, war on its way, disasters and death, matched exactly the mood of our late-depression and post-depression youth."[5] In her journal, she wrote, "Also many war dreams—almost every night. Tanks, lost in crowds of refugees, bombardments, etc." The navy's takeover of Key West in preparation for World War II beginning in 1939, which drove Stevens to abandon his former paradise for good, is similarly described by Bishop. Writing to a friend in 1942, she complains, "One poor old man committed suicide two days ago because he heard they were going to take his house....And when the war is finally over, Key West will be more ruined than ever—nothing but a naval base and a bunch of bars and cheap apartments."[6]

Dispossession, as the critic David Kalstone pointed out, moved her. The story of her early life may illuminate her sympathies: born on February 8, 1911, in Worcester, Massachusetts, she lost her father at the age of eight months old, and within five years her mother's sanity disintegrated; Gertrude Bulmer Bishop was permanently institutionalized, and Elizabeth never saw her again. Always in delicate health stemming from severe asthma, the child was shuttled around from one set of (poor) grandparents in Nova Scotia to the other (more affluent) in Worcester, then fostered by an aunt and uncle (again, poor), until arriving at Vassar College. There, she started out studying music and ended up a budding poet, introduced to Marianne Moore in 1934—the very year her mother died, unvisited, in the asylum.

Early orphanhood, ill health, itinerancy—these were to form, and deform, Bishop's character in heartbreaking ways. But when she decided to make her home in Key West in 1937, rather than stay in New York with her friends and former classmates, there was a fresh complement of grim circumstance to drive her to seclusion. In 1936, an unstable college boyfriend, Bob Seaver, proposed marriage; she turned him down. He shot himself dead after sending her a postcard that read, "Elizabeth, Go to hell." Then, on a sojourn in France in the summer of 1937 with girlfriend Louise and a beloved Vassar roommate, the painter Margaret Miller, the three women totaled their car. All survived, but Margaret's right arm was severed at the elbow. Elizabeth had not been at the wheel—Louise had—but she was haunted by a sense of responsibility for an artist maimed so cruelly; on top of it, she had been impossibly in love with heterosexual Margaret.

The trauma of 1937 can't be overstated. After the European tour, when Elizabeth elected to live in a village at land's end—the southernmost location of the United States, the last island in an atoll chain, closer to Havana than to Miami—it was because she needed sanctuary. Once, apologizing to Moore for seeming "remote," she quoted a remark of Margaret's: "Key West has 'such a beautiful cartographic presence the way it flies off the state like the arm of a spiral nebula.'"[7] Was this a conscious echo of the accident that bound them in trauma? In a haunting fragment of a prose poem, Bishop imagines the consciousness of the arm severed from the body: "So this is what it means to be really 'alone in the world!'"[8] In Key West, she could experience fully this feeling of severance. "On an island," she wrote, "you live all the time in this Robinson Crusoe atmosphere; making this do for that, and contriving and inventing....A poem should be made about making things in a pinch—& how it looks sad when the emergency is over."[9]

Meanwhile, both Stevens and Moore provided models of privacy that suggested her poetic art could be developed under the radar, practiced at a remove from social life and professional demands.

*

In 1941, Bishop wrote this description of Key West in her journal:

> Last night was a dead calm—so still I could hear every word the neighbors were saying & the conversation of people going by on the sidewalk at 3 A.M. woke me up. Mrs. A. says at such times at her house she can hear the conversation of people out on the boulevard—at least a 3rd of a mile away. It is frightening to wake up into such dead silence, & then hear everything. The acoustics of this town are very queer anyway,—maybe it is because it is an island—sound travels like that across the water. I had been reading "The Tempest" before I went to sleep—"This music stole by me upon the waters"—& when I woke up it seemed as if all Key West was a queer antique musical instrument floating in the sea.[10]

And in 1943, she wrote to Marianne Moore a description of a job she briefly took with the navy. She lasted only five days grinding binocular lenses: "the eye-strain made me sea-sick, & the acids used for cleaning started to bring back eczema," but was pleased to catch a glimpse of behind-the-scenes life in the Navy Yard:

> I was infinitely impressed with the patience of those men fiddling day after day with those delicate, maddening little instruments.... The foreman, who was perfectly happy spending 5 days adjusting one lens, or 4 hours on one screw the size of a pin, would look at me very mildly & say "Don't let it get you, kiddo." Some of the things we worked with were beautiful,

of course—the lenses & prisms, & the balsam for gluing them. Eventually I would have worked on sextants & periscopes & all kinds of wonderful-looking things I don't know the names of. However, the sea-sickness I experienced was not unique—a good many people can't do it at all, it seems, & while I was there every once in a while a sailor would get sick & have to go outside & rest a while.[11]

These two sensory experiences of Key West, the one an acoustic distortion and the other a visual one, come to stand as correlatives for the symbolic distortions that imaginatively recast the island in the poems. As the reference to *The Tempest* suggests, there is a magical protean quality to it, which Bishop must somehow reconcile with her realist-descriptive temperament.

This quality sets it apart from the mainland. In "Florida," Bishop could write in the key of Stevens—here is his florid humor, his peacock brilliance:

> The palm trees clatter in the stiff breeze
> like the bills of the pelicans. The tropical rain comes down
> to freshen the tide-looped strings of fading shells:
> Job's Tear, the Chinese Alphabet, the scarce Junonia,
> parti-colored pectins and Ladies' Ears,
> arranged as on a gray rag of rotted calico,
> the buried Indian Princess's skirt;
> with these the monotonous, endless, sagging coast-line
> is delicately ornamented.[12]

"Clatter" recalls the opening line of the opening poem of *Harmonium*: "Every time the bucks went clattering" and the list of shells' names transposes the sense of being "delicately ornamented" to the page, creating for itself a shoreline with its ragged margin. Later in the poem, phrases like "The mosquitoes/go hunting to the tune of their ferocious obbligatos" and "the poorest/

postcard of itself" lightly echo Stevens's trademark assonance, as in "Homunculus et la Belle Etoile": "The innermost good of their seeking/Might come in the simplest of speech."

Bishop relaxes Stevens's blank verse into conversational, free-verse rhythms that subvert the longing for "ideas of order"; they allow for the random and arbitrary with expanding and contracting lines. Her new environment was teaching her how to look at disorder without imposing an order on it, aestheticizing it. She wrote her in journal, "What I like about Key West is its *sketchiness*, its fragility—the wooden buildings laid so lightly together, in the midst of the dangerous, poisonously colored seas, full of man-eating fish, subject to hurricanes; also apparently liable to be forced apart and over-run by the strange plant-life, etc. Why didn't Stevens do more with it?—or was it just a name he picked up? I don't believe so because he is very accurate about the *sunsets* here."[13] What does it mean to "do more with it"? To go back to her perceptions of auditory illusion and vertiginous ships' lenses, we might take account of the ways that Bishop both acceded to and departed from postcard notions of Florida's Edenic floridity. Her peacock shows its colors in peculiar, less-than-resplendent moments.

Compare her poem "Little Exercise" to Stevens's "A Fish-Scale Sunrise." He says,

> Melodious skeletons, for all of last night's music
> Today is today and the dancing is done.

She says,

> Think of the boulevard and the little palm trees
> all stuck in rows, suddenly revealed
> as fistfuls of limp fish-skeletons.

Both poems are apostrophes: his is rhetorical, addressing symbolic skeletons; hers is personal, addressed to her friend Thomas

Edwards Wanning. His skeletons are metonyms for mortal humans; hers are real trees bedraggled in a storm. His sunrise mourns the end of the night's festivities; her approaching storm is "roaming the sky uneasily/like a dog looking for a place to sleep in." He says, more generally,

> The ruts in your empty road are red.

She says, more specifically,

> The boulevard
> and its broken sidewalks with weeds in every crack
> are relieved to be wet, the sea to be freshened.

Sometimes Bishop's realism takes the form of a fascination with ugliness. In various letters to Robert Lowell in 1947, when they were getting to know each other, she explained that Key West "in general...is really *awful* and the 'beauty' is just the light or something equally perverse." Using language that would find its way into her famous poem "The Bight," she continued: "The water looks like blue gas—the harbor is always a mess, here, junky little boats all piled up, some hung with sponges and always a few half sunk or splintered up from the most recent hurricane. It reminds me a little of my desk."

Later that year, "We had a small tornado last week....The sun came out in an hour or so & a friend drove me around to see the damage and the ships still crashing around in the bights. The streets of colored town were full of people all out walking around as if it were a holiday and everything had a chilly bleached look—but a dreadful mess at the same time."[14] Hence, Stevens's "jolly place—joli" from 1922 becomes the "dreadful mess" of 1947. But the "bleached look" is unexpected for a Florida landscape, and it harks to another one of her stranger perceptions—that of Key West's *dryness* between two seas, which her "water...like blue gas" intensifies.

This sense of desiccation is embedded in the etymology of Key West, Cayo Hueso, "Island of Bones," or "Bone Key" (which Bishop, incidentally, had planned to use as a title for an unfinished suite of poems). In a translingual homonymous leap, *hueso* ("dry") became the English "west," fittingly for the farthest island of the chain bearing westward into the Caribbean. The bones discovered on the island where the Spanish landed seemed to have come from an epic battle between warring Native tribes. "Key," of course, also has a ghostly association with bones, through Latin *clavis*, whence our "clavicle" ("small key") and the ivory of keyboard instruments, claviers or clavichords. (Bishop herself played and had a clavichord shipped from New York to White Street in 1939.)

An unfinished draft of a poem titled "Key West" begins "With a constitution dry as an insect's" and continues a metonym of "grasshopper-green and gray,"

> [Its mandibles] *rest*
> [Like the] dock-antennae here, [the] dry legs here & there,
> Carelessly {Casually] on the tepid water, [the] its rented room,
> Perched in [the] sun-lit, desiccated gloom,
>
> [In its??? thin-floored shelter from the hurricane,]
> Like a room with a riotous bar below
> doesn't sing, doesn't [save???], doesn't see snow.

And in the same journal she plays with the name of the island fortress out to sea:

> DRY TORTUGAS—find out why
> mixture of languages
> TORTUGAS SECAS?

She also further experiments with tropical "clatter":

> [the palms clattering like the beaks of]
>   …the pelicans " " " " keys
> [of a typewriter]

Palms like beaks, beaks like keys, keys like claves: the music of Key West is unmelodious as it is dry. It's significant that, quite apart from the human bones that were first found on the island, marine fossils—shells, teeth, fish skeletons—comprise the sedimentary coquina and limestone on which so much of Florida is built. She knew she was living on a compressed pile of *huesos*, a word that whispers under the tropical—and typewriter—clatter.

*

Readers may feel that Bishop's fascination with shabbiness was just a kind of slumming, particularly when she ventriloquizes Black voices; "Songs for a Colored Singer" is a notorious example.[15] Unlike Stevens, Bishop did not confine her Florida poems mostly to landscape portraits; she wanted to populate them, and because Key West was a socially and ethnically mixed town, she wanted to capture that realism too:

> Cootchie, Miss Lula's servant, lies in marl,
> black into white she went
>   below the surface of the coral reef.
> Her life was spent
>   in caring for Miss Lula, who is deaf,
> eating her dinner off the kitchen sink
> while Lula ate hers off the kitchen table.
> The skies were egg-white for the funeral
>   and the faces sable.

Bishop worried, in a letter to Marianne Moore, that the poem "may be banal, I can't decide."[16] Its chief ornaments—the rhyming stanzas; the metonym of black and white shot through the poem, which ends with a lighthouse beam in the night; the association of whiteness with albumen and coquina and blackness with expensive sable—lend it interest and dignity, but its ending peters out in the impersonal sublime of "wave after wave." It feels like a feint. She wasn't sure either, she told Moore in a previous letter, about "Jerónimo's House," which assumes the voice of a Cuban man describing his home in a district called "Jungle Town," near where she was living in a boarding house on her first trip to Key West.[17] "My house, my fairy/palace" it begins:

> Then on the walls
> two palm-leaf fans
> and a calendar
> and on the table
> one fried fish
> spattered with burning
> scarlet sauce,
> a little dish
> of hominy grits
> and four pink tissue-
> roses.

Placed side by side with other poems about communities of color, it reads like a piece of exoticism. But placed side by side with other poems about lowly homes, "Filling Station" and "Sestina" (which describes her maternal grandparents' home in their poor Nova Scotia village), it gains aesthetic weight. It is one of "Bishop's houses," "my gray wasps' nest of chewed-up paper/glued with spit."

Dispossession moved her, yes—at the end of "Jerónimo's House" we are reminded of the hurricane that could annihilate this fragile assemblage—but it can only take the middle-class poet so far. She was a liberal progressive, and her statement in a letter to May Swenson, scoffing at women-only anthologies, can stand in for her politics generally: "I don't like things compartmentalized like that.... I like black & white, yellow & red, young & old, rich and poor, and male & female, all mixed up."[18] Bishop bristled at the popular notion that she was "rich"; the whole point of living in Key West was that it was cheap in the 1930s, and it was, she claimed, the only time in her life when she could live completely off the small inheritance from her parents' deaths in order to practice her art.[19] Her own early dispossession—parents' deaths, blighted and sickly childhood, shunted between relatives, some poorer than others—was certainly mitigated by a Vassar education, European tours, and rich friends, as well as her small legacy.

While Stevens's Florida poems mostly dodge this impulse to aestheticize the poor, in 1934, under the same broad public pressure for artists to portray social reality during the Depression, he wrote "Like Decorations in a Nigger Cemetery," a poem in fifty parts that did not actually describe such a cemetery but took it as a "colorful" analogy for its own odds-and-ends miscellany: "The title refers to the litter that one usually finds in a nigger cemetery and is a phrase used by Judge Powell last winter in Key West."[20]

Though never referred to directly, Florida was the source for the poem. Powell later reminisced, "We were walking in Key West when I stopped to look through a fence. I explained that I thought it enclosed a graveyard, as some of the rubbish looked 'like decorations in a nigger cemetery.' He was interested when I explained the custom of negroes to decorate graves with broken pieces of glass, old pots, broken pieces of furniture, dolls heads, and what not."[21] Stevens was interested not in dispossession, like Bishop, but in vintage Americana and regional customs.[22] (The poem's presiding spirit, after all, is "Walt Whitman walking along a ruddy shore.") It is a philosophical poem, but nothing can redeem the casual slur in the title, nor can the analogy with the African American cemetery as a kind of collaged trash art stand unrebuked. By contrast, the singer in "The Idea of Order at Key West" and the mysterious "Ramon Fernandez" are almost certainly people of color, but their ambiguity, as well as their assimilation into the lofty metaphysical themes of the poem, invites open-ended interpretations rather than funneling readers toward a definitive, "may be banal" meaning as in "Jerónimo's House," or exploiting local color as in "Like Decorations...." It turns out there are limits to social realism as an ethos and a style.

*

Despite the ways that Bishop apparently departs from Stevens and Moore—adopting a documentary descriptive style, adhering less to stanzaic and metrical forms, employing rhyme more casually and randomly, making no great show of vocabulary—Bishop is still, at heart, a poet of peacockery. Her journals show an intense preoccupation with style and styling. In 1937, she wrote a doodle that could have passed as an *ars poetica*:

> Prose = land transportation
> Music = sea transportation
> Poetry = air transportation

"Air transportation" hearkens back to her acoustic and visual illusions. There was something about the air—poems are airs, as the Elizabethans used to say—a medium for feelings, as air is a medium for sound and light waves.

"Off and on," she wrote, "I have written out a poem called 'Grandmother's Glass Eye' which should be about the problem of writing poetry. The situation of my grandmother strikes me as rather like the situation of the poet: the difficulty of combining the real with the decidedly un-real; the natural with the unnatural; the curious effect a poem produces of being as normal as sight and yet as synthetic, as artificial, as a glass eye."[23] Elsewhere she wrote of her maternal grandmother's prosthetic: "Quite often the glass eye looked heavenward, or off at an angle, while the real eye looked at you."[24]

Such a stylistic prosthesis, of the real and the artificial, could describe Stevens's constructs of the imagination, or even Moore's chimeras. There was never a sense for Bishop that art was an uncomplicatedly realist expression; she sounds like Frost ("style is that which indicates how the writer takes himself and what he is saying")[25] when she writes in her journals: "It seems to me that of any work of Art a good 'balance' is 50% of its interest given to its subject matter, 50% to itself—i.e., the medium, the subject of its own style, etc. 50% to the idea, 50%, (blood tribute), to "poetry", "etching", etc...Of course they're mingled, the mind doing the work does not differentiate at the time—but—one must have the *trade* + the *tricks* in order to be satisfied."[26] She was thus an aficionado of the peacock style. Her three favorite poets were Charles Baudelaire, Gerard Manley Hopkins, and George Herbert. Her ear for seventeenth-century English was gratified by the stylist Sir Thomas Browne: "I should like to do nothing but sit all evening and copy off such sentences as 'That wee call a bee bird is a small dark gray bird,' or 'What word you give our knotts or gnatts, a small marsh bird, very fatte and a a daintye dish.'"[27] In a letter to her friend Frani Blough in 1938, she wrote, "Lately I've been doing nothing much but reread Poe, and evolve from Poe—plus something of Sir Thomas Browne, etc.—a new Theory-of-the-Story-All-My-Own. It's the 'proliferal' style, I believe, and you will shortly see some of the results."[28]

Despite her light touch with rhyme, she viewed it as a power, as her journals attest:

Rhyme is *mystical*—asserting, or pretending to assert, powerful connections between
                                        witchcraft
A method of magically interlocking ideas
making associations   [scarcely???] legitimate
                                             pretending

Like Stevens's profligate and prolix style, Bishop's "proliferal style" is a fit with proliferative Florida. While she did not write directly about peacocks, as did Stevens and Moore, I see transpositions of peacocks in the iridescent catch of "The Fish" and the strutting "Roosters" (which Moore suggested renaming "The Cock," to Bishop's chagrin).

Bishop first sent a draft of "The Fish" to Moore in January 1940; its account of catching a Caribbean jewfish in Key West was factual, and the microscopic eye she trains on it is characteristic of Moore's influence. But subtle metonyms that run underneath the surface deepen its significance. The fish is a "he," a veteran, and yet has curious domestic qualities, as if to be "decorated" at once like both a veteran and a room could be possible. He's "homely," she tells us, and his skin is like tattered wallpaper, a word she repeats twice. He is patterned with lime "like rosettes." When the metonym turns to "threads" and "lines" as Bishop describes the filament and hooks that have grown into his lip, it attests to David Kalstone's insight that "Moore sees her beasts as timeless studies. But in Bishop's work, time provides the plot."[29] The poet recounts one story about catching the fish; she must infer the story that he cannot tell from his "medals with their ribbons/frayed and wavering" and hooks that are also the fasteners on an article of clothing. Decorated in two senses, the fish has a double life, to which the poet can only have a partial, yearning access.

Also, twice she uses the word "packed": his flesh is "packed in like feathers" (here the peacock analogy comes closest to the surface), and his irises are "backed and packed/with tarnished tinfoil." The word "irises" foreshadows the rainbow at the end; here, what is actually "packed" is the double goddess of rainbows and messages within the word "irises" and within the fish's eyes—all of which will be *unpacked*, or sprung free, at the end of the poem. The famous epiphany—"until everything/was rainbow, rainbow, rainbow!"—is akin to the moment a peacock spreads his tail.

The tiny scales of an iridescent feather, related biomorphically to the fish scales and visually to the rainbow cast by sunlight on bilge water, all merge into a figure that is both real and illusory. Iridescence, whether in the fish scale or the peacock feather, is created by an optical illusion. There is no pigment. Everything is, indeed, "rainbow, rainbow, rainbow" and vanishes just as quickly.

"Roosters" is another poem rife with metonyms of showy male vitality—with a difference. Where "The Fish" was battle weary, and the poet's release of the creature back into the wild was a "victory," the roosters of this poem are both the real roosters of Key West (their presence was already legendary, and cockfights were a staple of island entertainments) and the metaphorical roosters of the navy that were taking over the island, gearing up for conflict. She has referred to it as her "war poem," and the language is more overtly Stevensian and peacock-like, as well as more violent in its decoration:

> Deep from protruding chests
> in green-gold medals dressed,
>
> ....
>
> glass-headed pins,
> oil-golds and copper greens,
> anthracite blues, alazarins,
>
> ...
>
> The crown of red
> set on your little head
> is charged with all your fighting blood.
>
> Yes, that excrescence
> makes a most virile presence,
> plus all that vulgar beauty of iridescence.

The monorhyme of the tercets has something of a military drumbeat to it, though the meter varies, with lines stretching out and snapping back abruptly. The poem starts out as a reveille, since roosters announce the dawn and the sky is "gun-metal blue" (she repeats it twice, like a volley). Repeatedly, we're given things "protruding," "projecting," with "sallies" and a blood-swollen penile "excrescence" on top of the head, as well as a "flame-feather." Even the word "broccoli," mentioned twice, partakes of the metonym. Its etymology means "shoot" from the Latin *broccus*, "projecting." It's where we get our word "brooch"—another decorative motif submerged in a metonym.

Marianne Moore recoiled from "Roosters." She sent the poem back rewritten (in collaboration with her mother, her closest confidante), bowdlerized of its references to a water closet and droppings as well as its most forceful imagery. Kalstone sums it up: "Repeatedly, adjectives and phrases that are emphatically violent or crude are canceled: the rooster's 'cruel feet' and 'stupid eyes'; 'torn-out, bloodied feathers.' 'A rooster gloats/over our beds' in Bishop's version is, in Moore's, discharged of some of its private, erotic burden.... Moore even turns the tin rooster that tops a church into a gold one."[30]

Bishop protested: she wanted to keep the "sordidities." She argued that she was being *accurate* in a poetic depiction of Key West in a bellicose phase. It was, after all, Moore's example that taught her the importance of accuracy. "Miss M. and Hopkins stand at the top of 'observatory' poets, surely," Bishop wrote in her journal.[31] It was this observatory aspect, of Moore, and not the *lingus unicornus*, that she amplified. She would even grow less enamored of Stevens and his imaginative recasting of the landscape. Reminiscing to Anne Stevenson in 1964, she wrote, "At college I knew 'Harmonium' almost by heart.... But I got tired of him and now find him romantic and thin—but very cheering, because, in spite of his critical theories (very romantic), he did have such a wonderful time with all those odd words, and found a superior way of amusing himself."[32]

The difference between the aesthetic lenses of a Stevens and a Bishop depends, then, on the weight given to accuracy of description in the real world, which at heart isn't about style or ornament, but about angles of approach, and temperament. Stevens was a romantic, Moore was a unicorn, Bishop was a realist. In 1970, James Merrill, a good friend of Kalstone's, wrote to Bishop that he and the critic

> have been having fascinating (to us) conversations about your work. He thinks he is going to do an essay on Pastoral (his field) and "At the Fishhouses;" and all at once we were talking about this knowledge from the sea; the seal's curiosity making the singer sing—each learning from the other; the dredge in "The Bight" rummaging below the surface...DK's point had to do with the reversal from the classical pastoral in which the poet addresses himself to a world; now, so often, the world is asking, touchingly or otherwise, to be seen (Stevens's sparrow who says "Bethou me...").[33]

There is a beauty to this insight that has a direct bearing on poets in the early twenty-first century for whom climate change, or its rapid species extinction, cries out "to be seen." There is a moral urgency in looking, in being an "observatory poet," if the environment as we know it is disappearing. Poets like Bishop help us to *see* better and hear more sharply, as if the lens-grinding job she held for a mere five days were subsumed into her vision and the nighttime acoustics of an island could alter her ear—such that by reading her, we might transform ours. If the Florida landscape, which struck Stevens as a paradise and Bishop as fragile and messy, was crucial in this regard, it must be that we return to our origins when we near the equatorial zone.

If this makes a pro-ethics of aesthetics, am I claiming that the ethics of Bishop's style is superior to that of Stevens's? In fact, his aesthetics of imagination undergirds hers, and our understanding of her poetry would be incomplete without an understanding of his. Realistic description is necessary, but for it to remain meaningful to us in the future—something more than flat reportage—we will continue to need constructs of the imagination to frame and contextualize it. Bishop's descriptions are rich with a shadow life of double meanings, substitutions, and displacements. She could flash her colors; she could also practice camouflage. The publication of Bishop's first book, *North & South*, in 1946, marked the beginning of her career as a major poet—and the end, more or less, of her Key West years. She sold 624 White Street just as air conditioning arrived at the local five-and-dime. Did she finally reach the point that Stevens had reached, when a sanctuary abruptly loses its protective aura? In a draft of an unfinished work called "(Florida Revisited)?" she wrote unambiguously, "Change is what hurts worst; change alone can kill./ Change kills us, finally—not these earthly things./One hates all this immutability./Finally one hates the Florida one knows,/the Florida one knew."

"I didn't go to Key West until 1937 or '38—just for a fishing trip. The next year I went back and lived there off and on for about nine years."[34] When I read this casual summary in a letter to Anne Stevenson, written less than twenty years after her departure, I'm struck by her brevity. In poems like "The Fish," she looked long and lovingly at life—and "let it go." She even made an *ars poetica* of it in "One Art": "The art of losing isn't hard to master." When she let Florida go, she went "further, faster." She went to Brazil in 1951, met a woman and fell in love, and lived there for fifteen years.

Would Brazil have materialized as a destination without that decade in Key West? It is one of the definitive legacies of Elizabeth Bishop's work that she brought the southern hemisphere into the scope of American letters, translating numerous Brazilian and Spanish writers, notably Carlos Drummond de Andrade, Clarice Lispector, and Octavio Paz. She contributed a book called *Brazil* to *Life* magazine's World Library imprint. She edited *An Anthology of Twentieth-Century Brazilian Poetry*. A substantial number of her own poems are set in Brazil, and despite criticism of her "romantic primitivism," the appearance of those peoples and landscapes in our anthologies and classrooms is a win for cosmopolitanism.[35] From Key West, she traveled to Cuba (as did Wallace Stevens), then Mexico and Haiti, before embarking on an ocean liner to São Paolo. Key West, as all the travel guides will remind you, is closer to Havana than to Miami. Even more so in the early twentieth century than in the early twenty-first, it was an interzone of foreign influences—Bahamian, Cuban, Spanish. The revelation of a global reality beyond the United States was a siren song that promised further travels, further marvels, and poetic inspiration in abundance.

Coda

One of the first things I do when I arrive in Key West is walk to the old Key West Bight, now known as the Seaport, which has been developed into a boardwalk of continuous bars/restaurants. The bight itself is impossible to get the measure of, crowded as it is with boat slips, yachts, and masts: I can't picture the shrimp boats and turtle kraals and canneries that jostled there in the poverty-stricken mid-1930s. It is murderously hot; the ice melts in my limeade within ten minutes, and yet there are large entourages strolling through the streets with piña coladas in their hands. It is summer solstice, 2021, and the last supermoon of the year is almost full. A shop girl tells me it's usually sleepy at this time of year, but every resort in America is currently doing brisk business: the nation has doffed its mask.

Then Arlo Haskell who runs the Key West Literary Seminar and is a knowledgeable reader of Bishop, suggests I bike out to the Garrison Bight: the locals believe that was the place where she wrote her sad birthday poem, which ends with the yoked mots justes for which she is famous: "awful but cheerful." In that phrase, I hear the distant echo of Elizabethan courtiers who reconciled wistfulness and lightness, resignation and grace. Philip Sidney, who on his deathbed at the age of thirty-one requested a dance tune, would have approved. We should number Bishop among the gallants, a style defined by the critic Donald Sutherland as "capricious play of mind...wit, rapidity, and swagger."[36] Bishop's gallantry, though, is less of a swagger and more of a bossa nova.

When I set out, the sky is darkening and lightning flashes a warning. I wait a little bit, and it passes. Then I ride down Fleming, left on White, and right on the road that takes me over a rising causeway that crosses a narrow channel. The character of the place changes; outside Old Town the structures look both humbler and tougher, more functional and well used. There's nothing frou-frou about the marina I pass on the other side, and bicycling along the curve of the lonely bight I'm irrationally convinced, mystically convinced, that this small, oblong, shallow, and dirty body of water is the bight. I can see the grubby, spongy sea grass on the rocky bottom, through yellow water, and I take in the low houses with their simple docks; on either end of the bight are small marinas with forests of masts that might well have suggested Baudelaire's "Correspondances" to Bishop—

> La Nature est un temple où de vivants piliers
> Laissent parfois sortir de confuses paroles;
> L'homme y passe à travers des forêts de symboles
> Qui l'observent avec des regards familiers.

On Thursday, March 24, 1949, the *Key West Citizen* reprinted "The Bight" (after its publication in the *New Yorker*) with the headline,

> Excavations at Garrison Bight Inspire Local Poet
> Unless one is still in the shovel and pail youngster set, or an incipient sidewalk superintendent, the sight and sound of dredging and excavations sets most people's teeth on edge—particularly in the early morning, when all one can do is vainly

cuss and gnash one's teeth, and try to turn over and sleep some more. Not so with Elizabeth Bishop, however, who has for many years been a popular Winter resident. Whether it's just because she is one of our more capable young American poets and writers, or because she is truly a poet—at any rate, she sees bits of the universe dredged up along with the "jawful of marl" and what's more sold her impressions to the New Yorker Magazine.

My bid for melancholy Garrison Bight, as opposed to Key West Bight, reminds me of Bishop's own pet theory—that the island in *The Tempest* was not modeled on the Bermudas, or Roanoke Island, but indeed on Cuttyhunk, one of the Elizabeth Islands off the coast of Massachusetts. Like Key West, it is the last in a westward-leaning chain of islands: land's end. She stayed there with her friend Bob Seaver in 1934. As she wrote to Robert Giroux in 1937, "It rather upsets me that they insist Roanoke is the island of *The Tempest* and not Cuttyhunk, as I dearly believe."[37] The heart has its reasons. The imagination has its biases. She kept "Elizabeth Islands" close.

5

James Merrill

Silver Springs and Manatee Kisses

On first meeting James Merrill at a conference at Bard College, Bishop wrote in her journal, "delicate face, pointed, gilded with freckles, slightly irregular full mouth showing beautiful white teeth with finely visibly scalloped edges—nervous effect. Nervousness repeated in a mannerism of occasionally wrinkling the nose to raise the small light-framed glasses—somehow modest & delightful at the same time—Small pointed freckled hand—."[1] After her death in 1979, he wrote a reminiscence that conjured her physical presence—a face, he recalled, "a touch too large, in any case, for a body that seemed never quite to have reached maturity. In early life the proportions would have been just right. A 1941 snapshot...shows her at Key West, with bicycle, in black French beach togs, beaming straight at the camera: a living doll."[2] It's striking that one of the first things poets may do when encountering each other is to make visible the body that he or she strove so hard to subsume into that other "body"—of work. Bishop hated to be photographed. She was notoriously reticent about her private life in her work and in interviews. Merrill's portrait goes some way toward fleshing out our acquaintance with her—a woman who liked to drink and dance and play poker, bargain for trinkets and decorate her houses (he visited her in Ouro Preto, Brazil, where she had named her cottage Casa Mariana after Marianne Moore).

So it's no surprise that Bishop's face looms "large" to the young acolyte who adored her; nor is it inapt that Bishop refers to Merrill's features twice as "pointed." The elfin quality comes through in his stanzas—they frequently come to a point, as in the old compliment, "rapier wit." They are also elfin, as in fey, susceptible to the uncanny if not the supernatural, and almost always rhyming. Recall that Bishop herself wrote about rhyme in her notebooks: "*Rhyme is mystical*—asserting, or pretending to assert, powerful connections."[3] Rhyme is a kind of pointing; its earnest faith in this material mysticism is also *poignant* (from the old French, "to prick"). And then there is what Merrill wrote for Wallace Stevens's centenary: "In a word, he pointed and still points higher than anyone in our century."[4] My edition of Stevens's poems contains the acknowledgment, "Wallace Stevens's *Collected Poetry and Prose* has been published with support from James Merrill (1926–1995) and will be kept in print by a gift in his memory to the Guardians of American Letters Fund, established by The Library of America to ensure that every volume in the series will be permanently available." This was a physical token of a poet's afterlife. After Stevens died, in 1955, Merrill claimed to have spoken with him through the Ouija board; like Dante being feted in Limbo by Ovid and company, Merrill accepted the laurel from his precursor: "He remembered meeting me and quoted me a line from one of my own poems. We had little to say. 'We are embarrassed,' he said, 'like guests who have met too recently at a party and find each other again at another party.'"[5]

If Stevens, Moore, and Bishop created one sort of aesthetic triangle bounding an imaginative Florida, Stevens, Bishop, and Merrill formed another. It is one of the stranger coincidences that just a few years after Bishop saw Ross Allen alligator wrestling, Hellen Ingram Merrill took her young son to see the same show in Silver Springs on an extended trip to visit her family. Unlike Stevens and Bishop, Merrill had roots in Florida—insofar as roots can be had: like its soilless soil, white sand all the way inland, the history of its settlers is shallow. Both Hellen Ingram and Charles Merrill (cofounder of the investment bank Merrill Lynch) were born and raised in the northeast portion of the state: Charlie from Green Cove Springs on the St. John's River, Hellen from

Jacksonville, itself a young city. At the turn of the century, it was a sophisticated resort, drawing down wealthy society from the north, but in 1901 the Great Fire reduced its charm and the clientele moved further south on the Flagler railroad. On Merrill's mother's side, his grandmother was a poor white woman from Fernandina, Amelia Island, the first sea island below Georgia, and she married a transplant from Tennessee. On Merrill's father's side, a "carpetbagger" from Ohio married a girl from a Mississippi plantation. There were ancestors who fought on either side of the Civil War, but from the 1870s onward, when economic opportunity was scarce, it was to northeastern Florida that they came.

Merrill's parents raised him partly in their favorite Florida resort, Palm Beach, on an estate called Merrill's Landing, which sprawled from Lake Worth to the Atlantic Ocean, with gardens and a sulfur spring that flowed into a swimming pool, scenery that might well have sprung from the "pleasure dome" in Coleridge's "Kubla Khan." Henry James, visiting Palm Beach in 1905, disdained the society shenanigans of "hotel life" but fell under the spell of a certain melancholy in its landscape:

> One of these gentle ranches was approached by water, as Palm Beach has a front on its vast, fresh lake as well as seaward; a steam-launch puts you down at the garden foot.... This brief excursion remains with me, at any rate, as a delicate and exquisite impression; the neck of land that stretched from the languid lake to the anxious sea, the approach to real detachment, the gracious Northern hostess, just veiled, for the right felicity, in a thin nostalgic sadness, the precious recall in particular of having succeeded in straying, a little, through groves of the pensive palm, down to the sandy, the vaguely-troubled shore. There was a certain concentration in the hour, a certain intensity in the note, a certain intimacy in the whole communion; I found myself loving, quite fraternally, the palms, which had struck me at first, for all their human-headed gravity, as merely dry and taciturn, but which became finally as sympathetic as so many row

of puzzled philosophers, dishevelled, shock-pated with the riddle of the universe. This scantness and sweetness and sadness, this strange peninsular spell, *this*, I said, was sub-tropical Florida.[6]

This landscape would reappear, dreamlike, in many Merrill poems. The palms that grew on James, "puzzled philosophers, dishevelled, shock-pated with the riddle of the universe," comprise one figure for creativity, mediated through another literary reference: Paul Valéry, whose "Palme" Merrill both translated and set as a plot point in his masterpiece, "Lost in Translation." Palms also loom large in his great "From the Cupola," a retelling of the Cupid and Psyche myth that begins with Psyche receiving fan mail from a mysterious suitor in a southern city "named for palms half desert and half dream":

> City half dream half desert where at dawn
> the sprinkler dervish whirled and all was crystalline
> within each house half brothel and half shrine
> up from the mirror tabletop had flown
> by noon the shadow of each plate each spoon to float
> in light that warbled on the ceiling   Wait...

This beautiful image, in which reflections are cast upward by the light bouncing off bodies of water and refracted through windows with almost supernatural intensity, is countered by Psyche's sister's recollection of decay, dust, and heat—"Poor Psyche you forget/ That was a cruel impossible wonderland"—where a royal palm cast "batwing" shadows, shed great swathes of dead fronds, and uprooted the sidewalk. Those shadows "trod" the sidewalk "as our nightmares us" and the sidewalk comes to stand for a kind of trodden serpent in which "LIZARDS ANTS SCRAPS OF SILVER FOIL" lodge and are dislodged.

Throughout Merrill's oeuvre, a paradisical vision of Florida will alternate with its polluted counterpart—as in the "half x half y"

trope that recurs through the stanzas about Palm Beach. In Valéry's poem, the palm tree is distinguished by its ability to transform desert into fruit and milk:

> These days which, like yourself,
> Seem empty and effaced
> Have avid roots that delve
> To work deep in the waste.
> Their shaggy systems, fed
> Where shade confers with shade,
> Can never cease or tire,
> At the world's heart are found
> Still tracking that profound
> Water the heights require.

In other words, the paradisical aspect of the landscape is the result of the palm's secret underground labors, sending roots out tirelessly, at great cost, until the payoff comes in the form of underground springs.

The mythography of Florida springs precedes the mythography of paradisical beaches—recall Ponce de León's Fountain of Youth. Inland, the springs are hidden in dense foliage, approached via thin, white sandy footpaths; they burst upon the eye as a rough-hewn turquoise blazing suddenly in a clearing, the pure rays of sun refracted upward through the emerald shadows thrown by pine and cypress groves.

Springs in Greek and Roman mythology were variously linked to poetry and prophecy, the Muses and Apollo, the Delphic Oracle and Pegasus. In the Homeric Hymn to Apollo, "the far-shooter" was born on "rocky island" Delos, with his mother Leto "hard by the palm-tree"; he defeats the nymph Telphousa and builds a temple on her waters; he kills the monster Typhon at Delphi. For the Romans, the Castalian spring sits close by the seat of the Delphic oracle; it is the "source" of poetry. The winged horse Pegasus, the figure for poetic inspiration, was said to have struck his hoof on a rock, thus tapping the Hippocrene ("horse's spring") on Mt. Helicon, the seat of the Greek muses, kept alive in English by Keats's famous line in "Ode to a Nightingale": "O for a beaker full of the warm South/Full of the true, the blushful Hippocrene." So accustomed are we to using "source" and "resource" as metaphors that we forget the literal meaning is found in bodies of water that bubble up from below the ground. In Florida, as in the Mediterranean landscapes of Greece and Italy, a limestone karst is filtered by rainwater that erodes deep caverns and underground streams.

Merrill's springs derive from the landscape of his childhood; his childhood doubles *as* his poetic spring. "Quatrains for Pegasus" is a candidate for his most emblematic poem in this vein, published in his final book, when his terminal disease must have become frighteningly clear to him. As the story unfolds, the child Merrill is taken by his nanny on Saturday mornings to a public park "on a parched fairway" (recalling Psyche's sister's impression of Palm Beach), where a fountain consisting of four horses (i.e., a quatrain) holding up the globe is animated with jets on the hour; the ritual is couched in the language of a covert religious rite. That is, although the tone is casual and conversational, the symbolism is acute: it is "Memorial" park (Mnemosyne, memory, is the mother of the Muses); the globe is fashioned from metal meridians that light and water sluice through; the child poet sees it as "global ribcage," a metaphor for the Depression. But the marble horses themselves mechanically miming a gallop through the spray (the hooves, of course, are a stand-in for metrical "feet") prompt the question:

> I wondered if passing through a white horse's head
> Was curing the municipal water for good
> Of its butts and tinfoil? Making trees toss with joy,
> Flagstones glitter and gleam?

The nascent poet wonders: can a life lived in art be saner, healthier, more virtuous? Would it "keep—for each morning paper brought fresh horrors—Our whole world from starving like the Armenians,/Its bones from coming to light like the Lindbergh baby's...?"

The kidnapped Lindbergh baby was discovered dead in May 1932; the poet would have been six years old. His nanny, far from protecting her charge, brings him in confrontation with cosmic disorder; her own brother "lay buried in France," a soldier who died on the plain of Verdun. "The more she said, the wickeder the world got." And then Merrill ends with the poet turning from his female caregiver to the virile chimera Pegasus with this naked prayer: "Don't let it, I begged the horses, get any worse."

The poem, seemingly offhand and anecdotal, turns allegorical on a dime. It kindles our childlike faith in fairy tales: a fountain is activated, a storybook character comes to life, and all of existence is elevated—redeemed—for the short duration of the enchantment. The poem dramatizes the ingenuous child, though we know it was the adult, dying of AIDS, who wrote it. He stays in the shadows like a discreet Prospero; this distance between the two versions of the man gives poignancy to the verse.

*

Charles Merrill, the poet's father and lord of Merrill's Landing, adopted a coat of arms featuring the head of a peacock.

> Consider other birds: the murderous swan
> And dodo now undone,
> The appalling dove, hens' petulant sisterhood;
> And then the peacock that no cry alarms,
> Tense with idlesse, as though already on
> A terrace in boxwood
>   Or graven in a coat of arms.

"The Peacock" appeared in *First Poems*, published when James was twenty-five; it showcases the flaws of a young poet besotted with words, and yet it's a perfect prototype of the mature Merrill poem: heavy with the burden of physicality, down to the thick materiality of the sounds. Merrill sympathizes with figures like the peacock, objectified into mere emblems, drained of their vitality: beauty trapped in museum pieces.

Much of *First Poems* concerns itself with the *rara avis*, from its opening gambit, "Black Swan," to "Transfigured Bird," "The Parrot," and "The Pelican." Stephen Yenser has remarked on "the commonplace observation that he began as a Fabergé"[7] and here the difficult ornaments of intricate syntax sinuously overlaying a rhyming stanza pattern combine with the metaphorical language to give an impression of frozen baroque grandeur. Words like "idlesse"—anachronistic word for indolence or "idleness"—tip the poem into mannerism. Merrill would always struggle with his tendency to excess. (Consider that in one of his very last poems, when he was dying, he figured himself as a gaudy Christmas tree.) Yet "idlesse" is allegorically Floridian, with its heavy, moist, and sibilant atmosphere: Stevens would have used it. Bishop, not. But on this point Merrill drew on Stevens; interviewed in 1968, he remarked: "You can't forego the whole level of entertainment in art. Think of Stevens's phrase: 'The essential gaudiness of poetry.' The inessential suddenly felt as essence."[8]

Later peacocks in Merrill's poetry would pay their dues to realism. In his long poem "The Thousand and Second Night," peacocks

> Trailed by, hard gray feet mashing overripe
> But bitter oranges. I knew the type:
> Superb, male, raucous, unclean, Orthodox…

But the most famous peacock in Merrill's poetry is Mirabell, one of the spirit guides he encounters in his long poem *The Changing Light at Sandover*, written with the help of a Ouija board. Mirabell—a play on Merrill's own name as well as the courtly protagonist of

William Congreve's restoration comedy, *The Way of the World*—is indeed in charge of instructing Merrill in the ways of the world on the other side of death. He is also a figure for male homosexual love—"Is there not something of the Athenian in the peacock?" The peacock seemed to unite the Platonic and the libidinous, the beautiful and the sordid, the "unclean" and the "Orthodox." He is "the king disguised as messenger," harking back to Boccaccio's biography of Dante, where allegedly the poet's mother, on the cusp of giving birth, dreamed of a peacock heaping laurels on her on lap:

> She saw a peacock in a laurel tree,
> Beak snipping the clustered berries—down they fell
> Until the skirt she held outspread was full—
> And woke in labor.

*

By the time the 1962 collection *Water Street* appeared, Florida came to be a fabulous backdrop to real histories: in a poem implicitly addressed to his mother, he envisioned "Your entire honeymoon,/A ride in a rowboat/On the St. Johns River,/Took up an afternoon." And in a tribute to his grandmother, "Annie Hill's Grave," he inverted Cape Canaveral: "The casket like a spaceship bears her/In streamlined, airtight comfort underground." He would revisit his grandmother again in "The Dresden Doll," the second section of his poem "Two from Florida": "Mis' Annie looks just like a Dresden doll,/People would say about my mother's mother." Was Merrill's preoccupation with the anomie of beauty—the ennui of objectification—bound up with the rigid stereotypes of the "Southern Belle" embodied by his mother?

> The doll, of porcelain like her little chair,
> Had panniered skirts and piled-up, powdered hair,
> But sat, as women did by 1930,
> Legs crossed, with a pert smile—the platitudes
> Of rotogravure—

It was a whole society built to shield itself from reality with platitudes. Merrill's question employs the inevitable rhyme: "Would we all harden into attitudes?"

The peacock in him was ineradicable; something else in him, however, recognized that hardening into attitudes was a professional hazard for a poet as for a society beauty like Hellen Ingram Merrill (let alone one who had been raised within the rigid hierarchies of the Jim Crow South). Langdon Hammer, Merrill's biographer, describes Hellen (with two l's, collapsing Helen of Troy with either hellion or hellcat) as having a "Cupid's-bow lips and cool fashion model poses, her hair pulled back tight in the helmeted style of a flapper."[9] She was no doll: she was a professional, an enterprising reporter, who as a young woman established a society newsletter first for Jacksonville and then for Miami, going on to New York and apprenticing to Condé Nast himself before meeting, and falling in love with, Charlie Merrill. The fact that they were both transplanted Floridians seemed like a foundation.

One escape from frozen attitudes/platitudes is through the ambivalence generated by words' polysemous perversity. Merrill was a master at this, as Yenser elaborates: "Merrill has been a writer uncannily alert to reversals and doublings. The duplicate and the didymous, the obverse and the inverse, the geminate and the specular are part and parcel of his art. Pun, paradox, alter ego, chiasmus, spoonerism, and all kinds of literary double-stopping and counterpointing are his stock in trade."[10]

As Merrill wrote, "Anything worth having's had both ways."[11] In addition to always living in two places—alternating between Connecticut and Greece, then Connecticut and Key West—he maintained his long-term partner, David Jackson, while pursuing short-term lovers. In "The Thousand and Second Night" he suffers an affliction called Bell's palsy, where one half of his face is mysteriously paralyzed; this happens to take place in Istanbul, site of the Hellespont—the ancient divide between Europe and Asia.

How did this sensibility develop? Yenser explains: "He surmises that his earliest literary efforts sprang from a need to reconcile the influences of his mother and his father, whose marriage ended just before his twelfth birthday, when he glosses a phrase he wrote in his diary, some time after the divorce, about Silver Springs, Florida: '"Heavenly colors and swell fish." What is that phrase but an attempt to bring my parents together, to remarry on the page their characteristic inflections—the ladylike gush and the regular-guy terseness?'"[12] This couple became a larger-than-life force of nature in Merrill's verse: "Father Time and Mother Earth/A marriage on the rocks." "The Broken Home" is his best-known poem about their rift; less well known is "Two from Florida," where "Green Cove Springs" stands in for his father and "Dresden Doll" for his mother. The St. John's River is what joins, or marries, them: Floridian waters thus provide not only the scenic backdrop of childhood but also the allegorical confluence of the two people who conceived him and who can't be unjoined in the body of the child.

All this is perhaps to say: What *is* a source? It is simultaneously an underground water spring, one's childhood, one's biological parents, inspiration for a poem; and it is the origin of a quotation or citation—this last perhaps a metaphor that can encompass all of these meanings. For what is a quotation but a repetition, a recurrence, a resurgence? Merrill made a game of citation and false citation—in "From the Cupola," for instance, he cites a made-up source by a fictitious author: A. H. Clarendon's *Psyche's Sisters*. "Lost in Translation" is partially about locating a copy of a copy— Rilke's translation of Valéry's "Palme," which, *pace* Auden, is necessarily a copy, because art copies nature, or the real. Between the ghostly doublings that haunt Merrill's wordplay and his story plots and the sheer indecideability of true "sources," we intuit a fluid medium in which the anxiety of death, or "drying up," is mollified by a recourse to ramification, those palm roots that keep putting out tendrils under duress and, with enough patience and faith, are eventually rewarded.

*

When, in the late 1970s, Merrill's partner David Jackson bought a house in Key West, Merrill was mildly annoyed and registered it in his poem "Clearing the Title." "God help us, you/Have chosen, sight unseen, this tropic rendezvous/Where tourist, outcast and in-groupie gather/Island by island, linked together,/Causeways bridging the vast shallowness—." The seedy aspects, though, were what would save life from the rulebound ethos of Palm Beach (where he visited his mother in later years) with its tennis whites, golf whites, yacht whites. The poem begins in skepticism and ends in a harlequinade as "the balloons...although tonight we trust no real/Conclusions will be reached—float higher yet,/Juggled slowly by the changing light." It's just like Merrill to think of balloons rising toward conclusions, as though poetic lyric is a gas, lighter than air, trapped in our heads!

When I visited 702 Elizabeth Street, I saw that its curb appeal differs from that of Bishop's house: it is one of charm rather than stateliness, with gingerbread moldings giving a flourish to the pillars upholding the steeply arched roof. It is nestled in shrubbery, ferns and a young frangipani, green and white to match the palette of the house front. Just outside the gate, the former owners' initials are scratched into the cement: JM DJ '85.

The current owner kindly showed me around, and the interior is much more spacious than it looks from outside. A long dogtrot partitions the house, with Merrill's bedroom and study on the left and Jackson's on the right. The house was built in the 1860s in the Bahamas of now-extinct Dade pine, my guide explained, and reassembled on the lot. The addition that Merrill put on in the back is a large, well-lighted space, with glass in the spandrels—rather unlike most Florida buildings, which are made to block the sun.

The pool right outside the addition used to have a gate around it hung with mirrors and a disco ball above. The place was built for pleasure, and there were parties almost every night. Merrill and Jackson hosted Leonard Bernstein and Elizabeth Taylor, whose voice coach owned a house on the same block. In this village milieu, no one was more than a degree of separation from a celebrity.

Part of what reconciled Merrill begrudgingly to Key West was its resemblance to his childhood Palm Springs—the light, the smells, the lizards. But something else was happening to his poetry, too. Having finished his decade-in-the-making epic in three parts, *The Changing Light at Sandover*, he found himself in that anticlimactic state of exhaustion that follows the completion of a major project—one that met with prizes, acclaim, triumphant success. What next? Merrill's aestheticism, so fully achieved that some critics complained he was running on fumes, alighted on the subjects of environmental degradation, ecosystem destruction, the disappearance of wildlife. It was the 1980s, and (mirrors and disco balls aside) the country led by Ronald Reagan was vigorously working to paper over the oil crisis and other disturbances, tamping down the uneasy growing consciousness of the limits of natural resources.

Merrill, child of Charlie, knew a hustle when he saw it. Florida was notorious for its real estate flimflam artists. In "Developers at Crystal River," he registered the suffering of manatees excoriated by boat propellers and other human-inflicted abuse. The poem begins "Elysian glade—" only to correct itself, "No, we are underwater./These are the Springs." The force of the flow from the springhead creates a turbulence that resembles trees—trees of bubbles—in a "glassed-in bower of bliss."

> The mother manatees,
> Brought here as babies, bring their babies here

...but it is not a bower of bliss when a boat buzzes by, and the water reddens with the blood of a struck cow ("huge, myopic"):

> Muses of sheer
> Indolence they are, and foes
> To nothing in creation

Here was "indolence," not the effete "idlesse" of the younger Merrill. The artificial rococo he imagined for his bored and encumbered peacocks is now the threatened habitat of a more homely, though similarly encumbered, manatee.

> Sweet heaven, here comes one—
> No heavier than a sigh
> Or small dirigible
> Gone limp, or adipose
> Naiad walking through murk, on knives. Unmarriageable
> (Unless to the Prince of Whales)
> In her backwater court
> She'll have escaped our human hells—?
> Look how the blades have cut
> Even into her.

The tongue-in-cheek pun is outrageous, but it's also an attempt to avoid (in his literal bathysphere) bathos: he adopts Bishop's "awful but cheerful" stance toward life and imbues it with a parental tenderness. When he compares the unprepossessing manatee cow to the Little Mermaid, who changes her fish tail to feet at the cost of feeling constantly that she is "walking on knives," Merrill wonders if the manatee's plainness recuses her from the ravages of love ("our human hells"), but sees that she's been damaged also—not by knives from below, like the Little Mermaid, but from above by boat propellers. The cheeky tone ("Prince of Whales") doesn't undermine the dismay and compassion; it extends the trope of the fairy tale—about which he is serious. At the end of the poem, the manatee seems to offer the snorkeler-poet an "unshaven kiss." It is he who has become her betrothed now: married by a rhyme. How the stiff, ungainly peacock cedes to the ungainly, tender manatee is one measure of Merrill's growth from young to mature poet: the Dresden doll figure, the objet, shatters, and the motherly bulk of the fluent manatee is matched with the raspy kiss of a man, elevating the maternal into something more essential than beauty, and available to either sex.

Coda

As an undergraduate at Amherst in 1946, Merrill wrote to his friend William Burford: "It is not inconceivable that one day we shall find in ourselves that all the contradictions and desires and angers have through their quarreling created a way of life, a way of thought, an element as lucid, revealing as many wonders as we had always imagined existing outside ourselves. We will have created our own commonplace, and whether we drown from love of it like Narcissus or find that it is an atmosphere accessible to the entire world it will be the achievement, of all others, that is most perfect personal and liberating."[13] Burford, incidentally, coedited with Merrill a one-issue campus magazine they called *Medusa*. The gorgon who turned men to stone on sight is the myth that figures behind Dresden dolls and precious *objets*; the symbolic work that Merrill must do as a poet is to dissolve rigidities, à la Pegasus's fountain, by creating "an element as lucid."

The Italian classicist Roberto Calasso speaks of "mental waters" as being the element of nymphs, emissaries of the gods. "It was this band of female and immensely long-lived, though not immortal, creatures who were to be the most faithful when it came to assisting metaphorphoses in style."[14] The nymph "is the quivering, sparkling, vibrating *mental matter* of which the simulacrum, the image, the *eidolon* is made. It is the very stuff of literature."[15] This description is uncannily close to Merrill's "element as lucid...and whether we drown from love of it like Narcissus or find that it is an atmosphere accessible to the entire world it will be the achievement, of all others, that is most perfect personal and liberating."

And Susan Stewart, in *The Ruins Lesson*, gives a capsule history of the association of nymphs with underground springs and grottoes, offering the luminous insight that "the fountain is the opposite of the altar—sign of depletion and sacrifice."[16]

So here is another facet of springs—not only do they evoke Pegasus's waters at Helicon, the home of the Muses, but also they are the element in which nymphs work their "metamorphoses in style." Meanwhile, the discharge at the springhead of a first magnitude spring in Florida can be upwards of 44,832 gallons per minute.[17] This is the habitat of dragonfly and damselfly larvae, called "nymphs," "living hidden below the water surface...unseen and mysterious." "No matter what type of water habitats they live the water must be clean and unpolluted."[18] They may undergo as many as ten or twelve molts as they grow to maturity—much like the draft of a poem.

It's not hard to see a Medusan aspect to the limestone coquina that surrounds springheads. It is ghastly gray-white, pocked with holes that give it the aspect of a skull. And, in fact, the shimmering blues and greens around the rapid boil are very slowly dissolving it. If the pressure behind the lyric impulse is great enough, a poetic line will *leap* like fountain spray. And it will dissolve bit by bit the clichés, platitudes, and stereotypes that harden in our mental waters.

6

Harry Mathews

Cool Gales

"But how choose the appropriate sticking point to start at?"—"Cool Gales Shall Fan the Glades"

As I'm driving down the peninsula from Gainesville to Key West—a five hundred-mile journey—there's a feeling of fatefulness about it: the general direction of fit in this state tends in a southerly direction, and the interstate that passes through my town takes me directly to the turnpike, which bears inexorably toward Homestead, where Route 1 takes over and ushers me to the end of the line on the Overseas Highway. Nothing could be easier. I don't need GPS. Instead, I'm using my phone to stream Handel's "Semele." It was not very well received at its debut in Covent Garden on February 10, 1744: it was the Lenten season, and this wanton story (*likerous*—lecherous—as Chaucer would say) of a pagan god and his concubine was highly inappropriate.

The recording ends just as I enter the city limits of Jupiter, Florida. Fittingly, a thunderstorm looms on the horizon, and a flash of lightning heralds the god.

"Semele" dramatizes the Greek myth, told in the Homeric Hymn to Dionysus and included in Ovid's *Metamorphoses*, of a mortal princess who was tricked by her lover's wife to ask him, the god Jupiter, to reveal himself in his true form. It bears a certain similarity to the Hellenistic myth of Psyche and Cupid (the basis for Merrill's "From the Cupola"). In that myth, Cupid (or Eros), the god, comes to Psyche in the dark and makes love to her on the condition that she does not ask his identity. When her curiosity gets the better of her and she lights a lamp to glimpse him in his sleep, a drop of burning oil falls on his skin and wakes him. She sees that he is the god Eros, but it is too late. He flees from her, vowing never to return. Psyche eventually redeems herself and wins him back, but Semele's punishment is severe and irreversible: she bursts into flame at the sight of her lover revealed. Only their son, plucked from her womb as she's immolated, survives: he is the god Bacchus.

Perhaps the most famous aria from "Semele" is "Where'er You Walk," whose verses are lifted from Alexander Pope's "Pastorals":

> Where'er you walk, cool gales shall fan the glade,
> Trees, where you sit, shall croud into a shade:
> Where'er you tread, the blushing flow'rs shall rise,
> And all things flourish where you turn your eyes.

Handel's music for the aria "Where'er You Walk" is renowned for its lyric beauty. The scene is situated in the middle of the opera and represents the peak joy of sexual love. That this is a profane, terrestrial, and even adulterous love makes it no less blessed: it is attended by zephyrs in a mountain glade replete with waterfalls and rainbows. This is the promise of pastoral poetry: heaven on earth. Swains and maids, nymphs and satyrs, panpipe-playing fauns—these fantastical figures and chimeras underscore the irreality of joy. That the pastoral ideal suffuses the eighteenth century to such a degree—evident in musical settings, in paintings of fêtes galantes, in architecture—reveals its function as the obverse of the liberal Enlightenment: the dream in the age of reason. That, of course, didn't make it immune from revolutionaries. They came for the queen of Petit Trianon, and the nymphs and satyrs did not emerge from their pictorial surfaces, nor could she hide in their pictorial depths. Pope's cool gale is a foreboding contrast to the fire of Semele's terminal love, and it will not save her, either.

Semele is one of my favorite myths, but I wasn't even dimly aware of the opera until I started delving into Harry Mathews's poem, "Cool Gales Shall Fan the Glades." I first read it—was bowled over by it—in 2014, when it was published in *Poetry* magazine, and it reminded me how intrigued I had been by this poet when I first came across his poems in a small pamphlet, *The Planisphere*, which I dug up out of a used bookstore somewhere in, oh, Providence? Northampton? Cambridge?—Back in the days of college towns with used bookstores, a kind of treasure hunt.

It's true that he is better known as an important avant-garde novelist, but now, in his eighties, Mathews had produced one of the most splendid poems I had seen in recent years. In early 2017, his death was announced in the *New York Times*. He died just short of his eighty-seventh birthday, in Key West, where he had spent winters for several decades. His collected poems came out in 2020.

When I first encountered the poem, I had only just moved to Florida. But something about it struck me as Floridian: It has the languid air of Key West about it. Nominally, it is an end-of-life reminiscence of a concupiscent boyhood, an address to a lost love. It is also a rich, long-lined sestina with an added constraint: instead of merely repeating the same end words, a letter is added with each stanzaic iteration, as if to mimic the snowballing of time: "at" mutates anagrammatically into *fat, fast, feast, afters*, and *rafters. Carnet de bal* transforms into *bail, basil, alibis, abseil I*, and *sibilate*. I didn't really notice it at first; the poem is so replete with sense memory, so full of appetite, that the sestina form deliquesces in its vocabulary:

> Delights often wreathed with unnecessary pain, like the
>   stout unforgiving thorns
> That tear shirt and skin as we stretch for ripe
>   blackberries, to be gulped down fast,
> Sweeter than butter and marmalade, quenching our thirst
>   better than sucked ice,
> Making us almost drunk.

I dug out my old copy of his selected poems from 1985. There, I knew, I would find poems that glittered with the dazzle of Mediterranean sunlight on sea: poems from a life lived in Mallorca, Spain, France. Mathews seemed the embodiment of an ideal: the man who knew how to live, or at least knew the answer to the question, "Where is that fabled place where *people really know how to live*?" ("People know how to live in this country," said Willa Cather of the French Riviera.)[1] It brought back my own peregrinations from one end of the Med to the other, days that seemed long gone and beyond me now, tethered as I was to work and parenthood. But the Mediterranean dazzle now seemed transposed to the lazy humid heat of the peripherally Caribbean Keys; had Mathews single-handedly airlifted the Muses from the Romans' *mare nostrum* to our own peninsula?

*

The sestina was first devised by Arnaut Daniel, the twelfth-century troubadour whom Dante revered (he appears in the penitential canticle, the *Purgatorio*, atoning for lust). Just as English has the plain and ornate style, Occitan minstrelsy had the *trobar leu* and *trobar clu*. Daniel was a genius of the *trobar clu*, the hermetic style allegedly full of games and difficult ornaments: metaphors, intricate stanzas, peacocking vocabulary. (The sestina was only one of the forms he pioneered.) Ezra Pound was a passionate advocate and wrote,

> The sum of the charges against Daniel seems to be that he is difficult to read; but a careful examination of the text shows that this is due not so much to obscurities of style, or to such as are caused by the constraints of complicated form, and exigency of scarce rhymes, but mainly to his refusal to use the "journalese" of his day, and to his aversion from an obvious familiar vocabulary. He is not content with conventional phrase, or with words which do not convey his exact meaning; and his words are therefore harder to find in the dictionaries.[2]

Petrarch called him "gran maestro d'amor," and Dante referred to him as "il miglior fabbro" ("the better craftsman"), also allowing him alone, of all the characters in the *Divine Comedy*, to speak in his native tongue. This macaronic moment in the poem exemplifies a *trobar clu* panache in double homage to Daniel. The troubadours played games with one another, inventing forms difficult enough to throw obstacles at their rivals and making of poetry a contest (Daniel and Bertran de Born namechecked each other in their poems). But like courtly love, which they also invented, the victor only wins an ideal reward: the love of the Muses.

Mathews wrote frequently in sestina form and nested allusions. "Cool Gales Shall Fan the Glades" doesn't announce itself as a poem about Semele, but the title is lifted from "Wheresoe'er You Walk," which itself was lifted from Pope by William Congreve for his libretto, subsequently adapted for Handel by an unknown librettist. The theme of Semele is hinted at and becomes a metacommentary about poetry and its slant approach to truth: "i.e./ Men and women kidding themselves that full-front-and-back nudity is the north/Star of delight rather than imagined nakedness." The subtext of the opening lines has to do with Georges Perec's Oulipian mystery novel, *La Dispartition*, which is famously written entirely without the letter *e*.

Semele wanted to see her lover Jupiter in his pure form—not in reflections, not god*like* (a *simile*), but as the god Himself. The idea did not occur to her until Hera, the wife—and goddess of marriage—disguised as an old woman, came to her, sowing the seed of doubt in Semele's ear. Who was the father of her unborn child? Come now, a god? In Ted Hughes's translation of Ovid's version,

> Jupiter should give you real proof
> That he is himself. Ask him to face you
> Naked as for Juno in heaven,
> In all his omnipotence and glory,
> The great god of the triple-headed sceptre.

When Semele asked Jupiter for a gift and he grinned, "Whatever you want," she said: "As if I were Juno,/Come to me naked—in your divine form."

Jupiter was appalled and wished he could take back his promise immediately; he tried to clap his hand over her mouth before she could finish her sentence, but to no avail; he had sworn by the River Styx. When he revealed himself to her as promised, she "burst into flame./Then her whole body lit up/With the glare/ That explodes the lamp—."

Or as Ovid says,

> corpus mortale tumultus
> non tulit aetherios donisque iugalibur arsit.

corpus, corporis N—body; person, self; virility; flesh; corpse; trunk; frame; collection/sum

tumultus, tumultus M—commotion, confusion, uproar; rebellion, uprising, disturbance

fero, ferre, tuli, latus—bring, bear; tell/speak of; consider; carry off, win, receive, produce; get

donum, doni N—gift, present; offering

jugalis, jugalis, jugale—yoked together; nuptial

ardeo, ardere, arsi, arsus—be on fire; burn, blaze; flash; glow, sparkle; rage; be in a turmoil/love

In these strange lines, Semele burned with the "conjugal gifts" of their love, as if she was penetrated with his thunderbolt in an act of electrical intercourse.

I love the multiple meanings given each word, as if a word is a prism and a translator must pick the right color from the many refracted from its spectrum. Mathews: "The alphabet's such a horn/Of plenty. Why cork up its treasure?"

Semele's misguided desire for Jupiter's "real" face is refashioned in Mathews's poem as a dismissal of "full nudity": "imagined nakedness, shudderingly draped like a fully rigged, fully laden ship without a drop to bail."

Homeric Hymn 7 tells the story of Jupiter and Semele's beautiful son Dionysus (Bacchus): how as a youth he was kidnapped by pirates. Once the ship set sail,

> But soon strange things were seen among them. [35] First of all sweet, fragrant wine ran streaming throughout all the black ship and a heavenly smell arose, so that all the seamen were seized with amazement when they saw it. And all at once a vine spread out both ways along the top of the sail with many clusters hanging down from it, [40] and a dark ivy-plant twined about the mast, blossoming with flowers, and with rich berries growing on it; and all the thole-pins were covered with garlands. When the pirates saw all this, then at last they bade the helmsman to put the ship to land. But the god changed into a dreadful lion there on the ship, [45] in the bows, and roared loudly: amidships also he showed his wonders and created a shaggy bear which stood up ravening, while on the forepeak was the lion glaring fiercely with scowling brows. And so the sailors fled into the stern and crowded bemused about the right-minded helmsman, until suddenly the lion sprang upon the master [50] and seized him; and when the sailors saw it they leapt out overboard one and all into the bright sea, escaping from a miserable fate, and were changed into dolphins. But on the helmsman Dionysus had mercy and held him back and made him altogether happy, saying to him: "Take courage, good...; you have found favour with my heart. I am loud-crying Dionysus whom Cadmus' daughter Semele bare of union with Zeus."[3]

Ezra Pound's Canto II retells the story with stunning beauty. The hymn bears a final message for poets about the inspiration derived from wine:

> Hail, child of fair-faced Semele! He who forgets you can in no wise order sweet song.

Hence, Mathews's ship and "hidden cargoes guessed at—perhaps Samian wine (mad-making!)." This, along with the lines in the last stanza about being "scorched by Zeus's proximity (or some such baloney," rounds out the references to Semele as the hidden figure of the poem. (Mathews's irreverent asides are part of the charm of his conversational voice, like the hairiness of the satyr.) His quotation of "To His Coy Mistress" is another bow to eighteenth-century genius Andrew Marvell, whose planisphere Mathews borrowed for his chapbook title, as well as whose green verges—in "The Garden" and other poems—surely foreshadow Mathews's Florida glade.

The sestina form; the address to the shadowy lady from his past; the argument against plainness or nakedness ("as if ideally expression should be limited to formulas like $x \neq y$")—all of it is so consummately in the troubadour tradition that one might forget that Mathews was a renowned figure in one of the most avant-garde convocations of poets in the past century. He is, in fact, frequently remembered as the first (and, for a long time, the only) American member of Oulipo, expatriate author of the experimental novels *The Conversions*, *Tlooth*, *The Sinking of the Odradek Stadium*, *Cigarettes*, *The Journalist*, and *My Life in the CIA*. (A final novel, *The Solitary Twin*, was published posthumously, in 2018.) Born in Manhattan in 1930—his father an architect, his mother an heiress—Mathews was a literary teen in boarding school, but when he went to Princeton, the stultifying milieu almost defeated the poet in him. He ran off and joined the army in 1948 and then the next year eloped with Niki de Saint Phalle, another refugee from the Upper East Side. He returned to university, this time to Harvard, dutifully to finish a degree in music. Then he and Saint Phalle and their infant, Laura, moved to Paris, where he studied conducting and she acting.

Paris was where Mathews met John Ashbery, then a Fulbright Fellow. It was 1956. Ashbery introduced him to the work of the eccentric procedural writer Raymond Roussel and this galvanized Mathews's literary imagination back into life. In 1958, he came into an inheritance and used a bit of it to found a little magazine named after one of Roussel's works, *Locus Solus*, along with Ashbery, Kenneth Koch, and James Schuyler. It ran for four issues and included their own work alongside that of Barbara Guest, Frank O'Hara, Edwin Denby, and Anne and Fairfield Porter, among others. (Hence, Mathews is considered a member of the New York school, which makes him a figure in *two* great avant-garde movements.)

Mathews credited Roussel with showing him that prose could be generated along similar constraints to a poem, which liberated him from the dread of "psychology." "Bye-bye *New Yorker* models!"[4] In 1970, Georges Perec was given Mathews's *Tlooth* to translate to help him out of a creative slump; a friendship was struck between the two men, leading to Mathews's involvement in the Ouvroir de littérature potentielle, which included some of the most illustrious names in European literature at the time, Perec as well as Raymond Queneau and Italo Calvino. Their goal was to revitalize literature via gamesmanship and create new forms with mathematical methods. While acknowledging his awe and humility in the company of these giants, Mathews was well aware of the elitist and sexist optics, writing in 1999, "Literature and game playing, literature as game playing....The words evoke a weedy figure: the playful writer...probably male, never young (although often juvenile), sauntering nonchalantly down sunny boulevards....*Faber ludens*—a little ludicrous, too; hardly dangerous; hardly serious."[5] It is a testament to Mathews's character that not even inclusion in Oulipo could shake the sense he had been imbued with—perhaps in boarding school, as an aesthete among jocks, or at home, as the rebellious son of a wealth-obsessed WASP—that being an outsider was the honorable position. Thus his commitment to living mostly in France for the next couple of decades, despite his belief that only a native speaker of English could understand his writing.

*

"Cool Gales" has something in common with an early masterpiece, which also shows us the dark side of Greek pastoral myth: the first poem in *The Ring* (1970), Mathews's first collection, is a tour de force of psychic collapse and recovery. It is called "Comatas," after the mythical goatherd so devoted to the Muses that he sacrificed one of his master's goats to them each day. Discovering the cheat, the master locked Comatas in a cedar box and jeered that if he loved the Muses so much, let them save him from starvation. When he unlocked the box, expecting to find Comatas dead, he found the goatherd alive and well, having been fed honey by bees the Muses sent to infiltrate the box.

Mathews said he wrote three types of poem, more or less: poems that emerged from life crises, poems of imagined worlds, and procedural poems and series.[6] "Comatas" is one of the life crisis poems. It was written in 1961, around the time Saint Phalle left him for Jean Tinguely.[7] In her memoir The memoir is titled "Harry and Me: The Family Years", she wrote that she suggested a separation in December 1960, though not a permanent one. There followed several terrible weeks of weeping and pleading, but in the end she left him and the children, and he would not take her back.[8]

Thus ended their fabulous years, a decade of mutual self-discovery, travel, and art-making—flitting from Paris to Déya to Spain to Provence, foraging for chanterelles in Lans-en-Vercors, dining at La Coupole or Le Bar du Dôme with Giacometti and Beckett and Joan Mitchell and Jean-Paul Riopelle.[9] *Harry and Me* (which is her memoir, but interpolated with his warm ripostes) recalls early financial precarity and delicious complicity: he was "an ardent feminist" who shared the housework equally; they devised antics straight out of a Godard film—visiting the Louvre daily for twenty-minute runs; seeing who could shoplift the most expensive item in a bookshop. But Saint Phalle suffered several nervous breakdowns (precipitated in part by insecurity: "Harry liked and needed to seduce").[10] Their two children, Laura and Philip, would come to resent their (very young) parents' disheveled approach to childrearing. However, she had found her calling as a visual artist, and he found his as a writer; each supported the other's creative growth not only in a period of youthful experimentation and excitement but also against a troubled background of parental rejection. Mathews's *père* not only campaigned against his choice to write but also tried to get the marriage annulled. His mother, for her part, pushed for an abortion when Laura was on the way.

Harry wrote, of this crisis in 1961, "I was totally lost without Niki and didn't know what to do. I felt hopelessly inadequate with Laura and Philip, in being able to take care of them and being able to deal with the simplest problems."[11] Out of this came "Comatas."

The poem, which unfolds in several polyphonic sections that shift violently in tone and rhythm, opens calmly enough with a strange species of ekphrasis: the description of a thermometer against a backdrop of snow. The narrator sees his face in the reflection of the mercury ball at the foot, and further exposition sketches the narrator's bifurcated existence: "For the stripe (which the mercury glass bisects)/Separates *Père Europe* on the left/And Centigrade side from *Notre Fille/L'Amerique*, the Fahrenheit column." (In a recording of this poem, Mathews mispronounces it "foreign height" before correcting himself.) The "baroque" thermometer is also a work of art: it depicts "dun elevator shafts" climbing up the degree marks, illustrated with Silenus, "Arcadians in blue jeans," nymphs, and—here is where the myth enters—"a hive/of wild bees":

> The upper floors empty but for a woodland
> Mist or smoke through which a woman
> Yellowhaired and slim is vaguely naked
> On the right—is it for her one wants to
> Test the cedar elevator-boxes
> That rise with the disintegration of icicles and lace?

The bees that fed Comatas immured in the cedar box were sent by the Muses; here the Muse is figured as the yellow-haired *fille* of Europe. "If we entered, I must do so in exile and imagine/America (and you, my remembrance)."

Mathews acknowledged that his "passions had been Eliot and Pound."[12] There is something of "The Waste Land" here, something of the Continental mountains and seasons and a hyacinth girl: "your hair muddles/The real and the false in such ambitious copulation....Our minds are debauched, and our bodies are balloons—." As the ekphrasis wanders into imagery from the Comatas myth, syntax starts to break down, and then the strophe breaks, also like "The Waste Land," into a different voice altogether:

> The little girls—sighs of tar
> I'th'giddy wheat. On hieratic mountains
> I raped the bright corpses of daemons,
> Tractors shuttling yellowly below
> O valleys. I examine my exact feet
> By Proust. Ladies, have a drink—shadows
> Wander in through your children, and swallows
> Spin quietly in the tender air.

The original narrator flickers in and out of hearing. The bucolic imagery is as gorgeous as anything out of Pound's *Cantos*—"her ribs/Flash like the Var where the bullocks drink/And woven ferns droop from the bank"—and it seems to me that the better part of these echoes of "The Waste Land" issue from the influence of Il Miglior Fabbro (Pound *and* Daniel) rather than Old Possum. The text continues to break character and to break down, as in this vaudevillian/schizophrenic exchange between American and French alter egos:

> *Jack* If A follows B, and I love you, find "me"
> *Jacques* If you're after me—who are you?

Jack How can a hard sleeper sleep with the light on?
Jacques (They bore me to death with their broad vowels!)
Jack When was she not a cunning stunt?

the tense of her tendons

The section that follows this is a fever dream, in one galloping run-on sentence, of the satyr Comatas being sexually assaulted and savaged by nymphs Amalmé, Critasta, Garga, Nanpreia, and Nycheia. Roberto Calasso, in his essay on nymphs, emphasizes that there are two sides to them, illustrated by the myth of Apollo's conquests of Telphousa and the Python: "Both protected a 'spring of sweet waters,' as the [Homeric] hymn says, using the same expression twice. And with both Nymph and dragon Apollo uses the same words when he announces his intentions. For both were manifestations of a power that had split itself in two, appearing now as an enchanting young girl, now as a huge coiled serpent.... To approach a Nymph is to be seized, possessed by something, to immerse oneself in an element at once soft and unstable, that may be thrilling or may equally well prove fatal.[13]

The hallucinogenic episode in "Comatas" draws to a lucid close in verse again: "You"

> followed your mother into our orchard,
> And with a disdain of years
> I watched you pick wet apples.
> My thirteenth year was on me
> When that sight felled and terribly folly undid me.

Mathews has spoken of his memory of first meeting Saint Phalle when they were in their early teens (though the *coup de foudre* occurred when they encountered each other again on a train, she now a gamine of eighteen). "Cool Gales Shall Fan the Glades" recalls something similar: "you became the plume/In the horse's hat of my lust. I was thirteen when we first danced together."

After the masochistic fever dream, another incantatory passage rehearses the man's attempt to "sever me from my appetent mind.... From the limn of her limbs/nor the way of her waist/ From the air of her hair/and the ease of her ears." The list of feminine attributes, like a troubadour's blazon, proceeds from aural echoes ("the asp of her clasp...the thump of her thumb" until the body *is* the language, and a new section proceeds from "Zum"— both a reference to Khlebnikov's nonsense language "Zaum" and the sound of bees. Here, it seems, is the heart of the myth where Comatas is kept alive by the honey of the Muses, the crucible of the poet's suffering:

    Zum

    Ha sawaram aoaf beaesarm

    Zu zwurmu
    Zehe essewearrmm eovv bbeeeezz

    Zehea
        zarozaarazinazg zasawasazm zaozof bzaezaezasz
                                      bezz

                                                    biz
        Desire's everlasting
                            s   f
            hairy   w
                                    a
      didn'd   oil enema a
       I'm sorry   a
                                     a
    made him bend over   drool

```
                          a                    a
       "nates"        rubberbelly
      bluntfaced     pubic shave    a              a
      20 juicyfruit please                   footless
                                                              a
         lined the Jews up   I meant    a
            masterhole       then I can't understand
                                         drilled              a
                                           l              Sieglinde!
           sorry
                                           l
         ptlaarplop    "wherever you are"    the machine       a
                                                of ──          taste it?
                                                                a
          know thyself    a mass of bloody rubbish
                          will never    junior
                 enis                                               a
                              that time you
             brown spots    Mrs Pemberton     lickle-lickle    a
                               kotex mirror  "I love you"
              with his truncheon       would have        a
                                 sorry                  a
               Tonto?
                               no underpants?!         a
              slime knife                        a
                                   urp    a
               The smell           r
                             m
                  golden
```

In the recording of Mathews reading "Comatas,"[14] we hear a second voice drone behind his recitation of this section: he utters the fragments of language (buzzing with *z*'s), while the *a*'s that swarm on the right margin are intoned as one long groan of agony. In the final, valedictory section, the narrator is restored to sanity (the lid on the cedar box lifts, as it were), and the girl fades away: "'Goodbye, sweetheart, goodbye,' she said, 'Kenneth.'" In essence, we have experienced the mercury shoot up the (phallic) thermometer and sink down again. The poem ends, "Comatas sang this as dusk came." Comatas, and Mathews, have survived the ordeal thanks to art; the poem (a stand-in for the cedar box) serves as a kind of temple of Asclepius where maladies are worked out through dreams.

"Comatas" owes something to Idyll VII by Theocritus, where the myth is conveyed in a song by the shepherd Lycidas in a contest between musicians meeting up serendipitously on a country road. This twisty, jaunty epyllion presents a story framed by a song framed by a story inside a larger story—of three friends wending their way to a thanksgiving feast for the goddess Demeter. How better to amuse the Muses than to relay the story of the man in the cedar box within nesting narrative boxes? Mathews's poem, too, proceeds in this way, as a narrator studying the scenes on a thermometer gets sucked into its Arcadia and undergoes the thrashing that Theocritus's Simichidas—to whom Lycidas cedes the contest—threatens Pan with if his beloved doesn't submit to him.

*

Mathews's early poems are born of Mediterranean breezes. The pastoral *locus amoenus* is closely associated with marriage, as in "The Pines at Son Beltran," written in 1954 when Mathews and Saint Phalle lived in Déya, where they had their second child (and asked their friend Robert Graves to name him). "The Relics" is a set of variations on imaginary landscapes in yellow and red, bringing to mind the Phrygian Midas (Ovid, too, described a landscape turning to clanking metal), as well as, perhaps, the Phrygian mode:

> Where are the brass islands?
> There are the brass islands.
> Their yellow wheat does not bend, and their peaks
> Ring, flat. Their brass ports
> Have a stupid glory in thin dusk—
> By day, even near-yellow scrap copper
> In that drab gold is sweet relief.
> Streets are stiff with the wink and clink

> Of wired lids, a deaf clatter
> Of brass feet that batter brass,
> Brass teeth, brass tears,
> Brass breasts! In one such city
> I mound a mop of red rags
> But left, my business done. I forget
> The color. It is dazzling here to see poppies—
> Wild poppies salt the harvest wheat
> Like memorial ribbons red among tubas.

Painterly, suave yet *éblouissant*, these lines strongly recall Wallace Stevens. "Deaf clatter" echoes the first line of the first poem in *Harmonium*, "Every time the bucks went clattering"; "stupid glory," echoes the "stupid afternoon" in "Hibiscus on the Sleeping Shores," and the red rags and poppies recall the "red weather" in the last line of "Disillusionment of Ten O'Clock." (I wagered to myself that there must be tubas somewhere in Stevens—sure enough, thanks to the online concordance, I can confirm that tubas make an appearance in "Notes toward a Supreme Fiction.") In the third section, Mathews makes his homage abundantly clear:

> I miss the pink-eared angels,
> And the heartfelt noise of harmoniums at dusk
> Interwoven with cauterwauls; the garden too
> Is grime where the earth fluttered with tearbanes,
> Fustre, elgue, and tender paperdews
> Sweetening the souls of hot cigars.

This flash of Wallace Stevens's Key West foreshadows Mathews's move to the island in his later years. I started to develop an *idée fixe* about Mathews and his composition of "Cool Gales Shall Fan the Glades" in the setting of Key West, importing Mediterranean myth with the mediation of Stevens's "harmonium," kin to Bishop's clavichord and Handel's harpsichord. When Mathews ends his poem, "and every hidden woodworm wake from its dream to fall forever from the rafters," I think of *vers* meaning *worm* in French and, of course, earworms. It is also an echo of his source in Pope: "And headlong streams hang list'ning in their fall!"

Like Lycidas in Idyll 7, Mathews the poet was nothing if not a musician who ceded the contest. In his marvelous essay "The Monkey at the Wheel," he describes his earliest aesthetic experience at the age of nine or ten: being smitten with Wagner. He listened obsessively to all of the leitmotifs from the *Ring* cycle, collected and arranged in chronological order on a pair of old 78s; each leitmotif was named and stood for a concept; only the boy was confused when the very same motif for "Renunciation of Love (*Entsagungsmotiv*)" in *Das Rheingold* was reused in *Die Walküre* where Siegmund *embraces* doomed love. How can a musical phrase mean two opposite things? This conundrum leads into a long and intricate examination of the imbrication of words and music. (Incidentally, see the ejaculation of "Sieglinde!" in the bee section of "Comatas," invoking the impossible sister-lover in Wagner's myth.) Words, too, can mean opposite things and look in different directions at once; while this is a minority interest among those who wish language to communicate pure and simple, it is of consummate interest to poetic peacocks. Mathews might have given up music, but he gained its sister art.

Or poetry was really just the music going underground. In the procedural poems, above all, you see how appealing sheer permutation was to him. The fourteenth-century composers of *ars nova* particularly fascinated Mathews; in his description, "they would create music in which thirteen notes would be played against nine notes which would be played against five notes—things that are hard to figure out even on the page. Studying *ars nova* was an immersion in a nonromantic and nondramatic way of creating music."[15]

He pursues this mode in long satiric poems like "Trial Impressions," where he takes a song from John Dowland's *Second Booke of Ayres* ("Deare, if you change, Ile never chuse againe"), creating thirty permutations with titles that explain the approach: "Up to Date," "Multiple Choice," "Male Chauvinist," much like Raymond Queneau's *Exercises in Style*, which puts a bland anecdote about a bus ride through a hundred stylistic departures. Likewise, "Selected Declarations of Dependence" creates "perverbs," cutting and pasting the halves of different proverbs together: "Sticks and stones may break my bones, but words lead to Rome:'Red sky at night, do as the Romans do—/Rome wasn't built in a storm....'/When in Rome, gather no moss:/All silver linings lead to Rome." But my favorite work of theme and variation is "Marriage of Two Minds: Received Visions," composed of ten Shakespearean sonnets with comic rhyming—Byron via the Cole Porter songbook:

> He dreams another life, another guise
>   She dreams her lover is the young John Keats
> She dreams of singles bars she used to cruise
>   He dreams of being the late, and later, Yeats
>
> She dreams of next week's secret rendezvous
>   He dreams of Zen—withdrawing and detaching
> He dreams of flaunting his superior nous
>   She dreams she'll have that boy who's set her aching
>
> He dreams she dreams he's dreaming bigamy
>   She dreams of Renoir and no need to diet
> She dreams her loves are transient, young, and gamy
>   He dreams he excites girls slim as Juliet
>
>   Caressing her, he dreams of books he'll read
>   Caressing him, she dreams of books she's read

Mathews needed form to be "nonromantic and nondramatic"; he approved "noncommittal writing"; he warred against his own proclivities: "there's always an element of personal dramatization in everything that I write, and that is typically American."[16] Yet, "at its best, it's gorgeous," he said of *ars nova*, and the thrill of Mathews's poetry lies in its subversive gorgeousness without apology—and maybe, too, in the near-masochistic pressure of a temperament disciplining itself. The *Collected Poems* contains many forms—centos, translations, haikus, détourements, instruction poems, limericks, invented "lost" manuscripts, incantations, and works whose underlying methods or structures remain mysterious.

But always it returns to sestinas. Mathews's last, ambitious, and unfinished poem was to have been a double sestina called "The Politicians' Antic Spoil." Sir Philip Sidney's double sestina "Ye goatherd gods…" was an inspiration, but instead of merely doubling the usual length, Mathews was aiming for a mirror or palindromic effect, while also making the end words subtractive by a letter in each iteration, until the hinge, when the second sestina would build the end words back up again. Even at his most recondite and puzzle-loving, Mathews was—like Sidney, like Dowland, like the troubadours—a gallant. When given a memoir by the French writer Marie Chaix to translate into English, he fell in love with her story—and her author photo. "I wrote her a four-page handwritten letter using every writer's wile I could muster. I was about to mail this letter and then I thought, I can't do it.… I thought, This is too heartrending a book to use as a pretext for a seduction. So I threw out the letter, and I wrote her another one, ten lines in the simple neutral style only French can attain.…And it was typed, not handwritten."[17]

It worked. And after they married in 1992, she returned the favor, translating his novel *Cigarettes* into French. "For me," he concludes, "this proved definitively that classicism is far superior to expressionism as a way of getting results."[18]

*

If Mathews imported the Mediterranean, or superimposed it on Key West, this is a significant act of poetic magic. As James Merrill put it, "a culture without Greek or Latin or Anglo-Saxon goes off the gold standard."[19] By opening a line of communication between the Greek gods and the Keys, Mathews brought the region into imaginative contact with the richest, most durable treasury of poetic inspiration we have.

Marie Chaix was in Paris when I arrived in Key West in late June, but I was given permission to tour their house on Grinnell Street, right off the old cemetery. Like the other poets' houses, it has a short, white picket fence that comes to seem like an ideal frame: neither tall enough to hide the facade from view nor sturdy enough to provide security, it asserts a boundary in a friendly way.

And here, no doubt about it, is the cool glade of the poem. There are tall, swaying palms fanning like great plumes; there is color: a ti plant, a pink hibiscus, a red ixora. There is fragrance: a mature, graceful frangipani tree with blossoms as white as the fence, cascading down. (It is even more fragrant at night, to lure sphinx moths—tricking pollinators to visit: it has no nectar.)

"All this was Harry." A family friend who serves as caretaker in the summers tells me that Mathews took great care with the landscaping and had a hand in the design of the grounds. The modest look of the facade is deceptive: over time, a neighboring property had been acquired, so that there were two pools and three small houses. Two of them served as his and Marie's writing studios. ("And where he kept his piano.") The wading pools are nestled among banana trees, mango, mahogany, bamboo, and elephant ears. Orchids are trained on palm trunks.

From a balcony, I beheld the tin roof and unpainted vertical boards of the cottage where Mathews wrote. "Harry and Marie never changed anything; all of this is original." It's very Old Florida, I noted, and dark—built to keep out the harsh sun. The bohemian mingling of humble natural materials with objects of great value—oriental rugs, paintings and prints—felt very familiar to me, though I would never have the means to live like this myself. It was, possibly, a bygone era I was beholding—the taste, predilections, and connoisseurship of a vanishing generation, our last link with the European art tradition. "Our sweet love!" my guide called Mathews, wistfully. Why Key West? I asked her. "There were kindred spirits," she replied.

I chided myself for thinking I could discover or prove something by coming to Harry Mathews's house, standing in the presence of his writing studio. What he set to paper was infinitely more suggestive—already it had sent me to Handel, to Congreve, to Pope, to Theocritus, to the Homeric Hymns. I read an homage to Stevens in his macaronic line "where the flourished vowel lends such panache to your *carnet de bal*" ("Panache upon panache, his tails deploy": "The Bird with the Coppery, Keen Claws") and "I still bear your plume." If I was looking to be struck by lightning, wasn't this a little close for comfort?

"A poet is a man who manages, in a life of standing out in thunderstorms, to be struck by lightning five or six times." Randall Jarrell said that, during a more heroic era for poetry than the present one. It was also the most self-destructive generation of poets in history—the Confessional poets. Mathews, anti-Confessionalist, lived to a grand old age, and his demands were modest. He wrote gorgeously, but unlike Semele, he did not ask to see the full-frontal god. He embedded procedures and formulas into his work but did not expect his readers to deduce them like keys to a puzzle. He asserted the value of glimpses; he prized the intuitive.

The poet who sits down at the blank page wants to see where *it* will take *her*, not where *she* will take *it*. This is the crux of the practice. It's what the poet means in Cocteau's film, *Orphee*: "Etonnez-moi!" The poet wants to astonish and be astonished: by a fresh word, a strange rhyme, an original juxtaposition, an unexpected double-dealing. This is just a yearning for theophany by other means.

Or you could call it a yearning for total artistic autonomy—to *be* the god. To be independent of public opinion, of market demands, of agendas set by grant-giving foundations. What

Mathews had in common with Stevens, Bishop, and Merrill, besides Florida, was means. To write the poetry they did, peacock poetries of aesthetic independence, required money.[20] "Freedom is never free," the British writer Deborah Levy points out. "Anyone who has struggled to be free knows how much it costs."[21]

"Is this that fabled place where people *really know how to live*?" If so, I thought, biking around Key West's Old Town, you need a least a cool mil. Of course I wanted to resist this conclusion.

Epilogue

Laura Riding Jackson

I noticed the atmospheric effects before I read the news about Sahara dust arcing in a plume across the Florida skies. As sand from North Africa blows across the Atlantic, it sucks the moisture out of the air over the tropics and prevents hurricanes from organizing. It also contributes to spectacular blood orange sunsets. But what I first noticed was the strange blend of haziness and clarity, dust but also light refraction. I went on a walk at dusk to observe the luminous effects not in the west, but in the east, where a buildup of clouds acquired a strange intensity, strong outlines, and hyacinthine colors. They were hit by the rays across the horizon in strange directions, so it looked as though three fairy-bright suns were rising while our red dwarf set in the west. And then, as I fixed my eyes on the clouds, I saw interior arcs of lightning like synapses, and the clouds appeared to me as massive floating brains—a kind of wetware.

It was through Stevens, Moore, Bishop, Merrill, and Mathews that Florida parlayed its lush biodiversity into the language of modern American poetry. But there was also a poet who moved here in 1943 after giving up her vocation for good, and for almost fifty years Florida sheltered her silence. Laura Riding Jackson and her husband Schuyler Jackson, a historian, retired to Wabasso, midway down the Atlantic coast, to grow a citrus business and write a six hundred–page treatise on linguistics, *The Dictionary of Rational Meanings* (ultimately published as *Rational Meaning: A New Foundation for the Definition of Words*). They lived without electricity, running water, or phone service for decades. When he died in 1968, she lived alone and slept with a shotgun. After her death in 1991, her small cracker house was moved to Vero Beach, where it is open to the public much of the year and hosts a creative writing group.[1]

It's ironic that Laura Riding Jackson should prove a muse to new writers: she had broadcast her renunciation of poetry in a BBC interview in 1962, though it was clear she had stopped publishing verse much earlier. There is speculation that she burned her manuscripts in a ritual bonfire in 1941 in New Hope, Pennsylvania, when she and Schuyler were about to be married. He was a failed poet himself; it seemed as though she was committing herself fully to being Mrs. Schuyler Jackson by this gesture. She later wrote to a young poet who had inquired after her work that her poems were a relic from the past.[2] She had found personal happiness.

Laura Riding Jackson was the bad fairy of Modernist poetry, denouncing it exactly for the peacock traits celebrated in this book: "Ultimately, in the human production and enjoyment of poetry, poetry proves good only for itself. It provides something to admire—to do which may be argued to be useful and also argued to be an empty justification for its existence." What she sought in its stead was *truth*—"literally, literally, literally, without gloss, without gloss, without gloss."[3] Even before she gave up poetry for good, she authored (and sometimes coauthored, with her partner, the English poet Robert Graves) an array of diatribes, indictments, and interdictions against the current state of poetry. *Contemporaries and Snobs*, from 1928, suggested that Emperor T. S. Eliot wore no clothes: "Can it be that the social backing of contemporary poetic gentlemanliness is only, after all, a gloomy medley of scholastic anthropology, spaded Freudianism, Baroque Baedeckerism, sentimental antiquarianism, slum-and-boudoir philology, mystical Bradleyanism, tortoise-shell spectacled natural history, topee'd comparative religion and Arrow-collared Aristotelianism?"[4] This is the kind of criticism that invites social death—especially from a woman. William

Carlos Williams called her "a prize bitch."[5] But she was defiant: "Indeed," she wrote to Kathleen Raine in a letter found among her unpublished papers, "I have not renounced membership in the brotherhood because I never joined it. I was merely a woman who spoke her mind by the limited graces of liberty of which poetry has been the historical licenser-substitute for the ultimate generosity of truth, whose gift of perfect freedom is our own to ourselves."[6]

Social disapprobation wasn't the worst of it; her combativeness and her critical drive toward purity destroyed the poet in her.

*

It is a powerful conceit: the poet who falls silent. Like Arthur Rimbaud, another repudiator, Riding Jackson slipped away to a warm climate and lived as a stranger in primitive circumstances: a hermit in the lushest of deserts. And like Rimbaud reveling in the exoticism of Muslim North Africa, the Jacksons marveled at the Seminole Indians who manned the market stalls at Vero Beach in colorful garb and fantastic jewelry. This poetic silence is intensified by the idyllic setting of citrus groves and ocean, which had sparked Stevens's immortal line, "She sang beyond the genius of the sea." Her biographer, Deborah Baker, reports, "Laura and Schuyler survived hurricanes, droughts, early freezes, mosquitoes, bouts of depression, and threats of bankruptcy."[7] But the hardships seem to have channeled Riding's contentious energy, which threatened to lash out at any time, against herself and others, and which had made her so destructive in her previous life—so destructive that she once threw herself out of a fourth floor window, prompting Graves to throw himself out of another window (both survived).

Riding Jackson's 1986 preface to what would eventually be *Rational Meaning: A New Foundation for the Definition of Words* contains a hint of her feeling for Florida. Praising her assistant, a young local woman, in her acknowledgments, she remarked, "I think that perhaps my and the book's needs, and her store of capabilities, were made, if not in heaven, for each other, at least in Florida—which secretes an earthly providential beneficence the hiding-places of which have not all been dismantled by the destroying angels of civilization."[8] Going on to acknowledge her debt to the library at the University of Florida, she clarifies:

> But what I have done of work of writing, and study for writing, in my Floridian home-place, has been done in a naturally discovered, naturally offered, freedom of privacy. What has been done here need make no trouble for anyone of concern with what to do about it as matter for report. It has been done as nobody's business except as it might be found to be everybody's business. My husband and I were let be—left alone to be, left alone to do—by the Floridian version of the nature of nature, which, I think, is, in its essential universality, to let be, and let do. I have clung to the protection of my acreage-portion of Floridian universality.[9]

So it was freedom, simplicity, privacy—even secrecy—that Riding Jackson found in Florida: the secrecy required for the gestation of a magnum opus. Enveloped behind high walls of foliage, she felt nature as a "beneficence," gators and snakes less of a threat than the literary snoop. *Rational Meaning* was written as a rebuke to poets whom she accused of writing under a rhetorical and musical and pavophile enchantment, rather than as clear-eyed communicators of ideas. Plato said as much. In effect, Riding Jackson jettisoned poetry to become a philosopher.

*

Who was this woman who wrote "Poetry has been, and still is somewhat, an object of worship, an idol"? What was she running away from? She was born Laura Reichenthal to Jewish immigrants from Galicia in New York in 1901. She married at nineteen and started publishing poetry as Laura Riding Gottschalk—"Riding" was her own invention, and it saw her through various incarnations. Her early poems were taken up, and celebrated, by the Nashville-based "Fugitive" poets Allen Tate and John Crowe Ransom. When she divorced Louis Gottschalk in 1925, she frequented bohemian circles in New York as Laura Riding, befriending Hart Crane, among others. Then, at the instigation of Robert Graves, who admired her poems in *The Fugitive* (where he also published), she moved to London, into his household, and entered into a ménage with him while his wife Nancy decamped to a houseboat on the Thames with their children. Riding's first book, *A Close Chaplet*, was published by Leonard and Virginia Woolf's Hogarth Press.

The romantic escapades of that generation are well known—it was the era of polyamory *avant la lettre*—but the instability of these arrangements took its toll. The suicide attempt occurred after a histrionic scene with Graves and another paramour. She didn't kill herself, but she broke her spine and took many painful months to recuperate. Then she and Graves whisked themselves, and their literary collaborations, away to Deyá in Mallorca, where they remained until the Spanish Civil War broke out in 1936. This is where she seems to have written much of her work—poems, stories, essays—and where she and Graves collected disciples and fired off manifestoes and vilifications of literary trends. Her theory of "poetic sense" in *A Survey of Modernist Poetry* would go on to spur William Empson's *Seven Types of Ambiguity*, a landmark text in the creation of the New Criticism.

It seemed Laura Riding was destined to be an agitator, a gadfly, a palinodist. She was grandiose: "During my career as a poet I became increasingly an advocate of poetry," she wrote; "in the final stages of that career I claimed, I think, more than any one has ever claimed for it."[10] She was paranoid: when a young Wystan Auden claimed her as a huge influence, she and Graves accused him of theft. Later, after she left Graves, she also accused *him* of stealing her ideas wholesale for *The White Goddess*. In her essay

"The Promise of Words," where she lays out her objections to poetry, she claims that her acolytes misunderstood her; whereas she, too, had failed to transcend the limitations of poetry, she had at least understood the problem; her followers did not. "I laboured to discover the obscured coherences of the common language: from that came my linguistic strangeness as a poet, not from my speaking, after the manner of my fellow modernists, a language of my own—and came also my having an influence on the word-craft of many poets." However, "My word-ways seemed to extract more 'poetry' from language. But I only extracted more language from language."[11] Riding Jackson started restricting access to her work and refused to let much of it be republished, at least without an updated disclaimer, admonition, or disavowal. When scholars and editors tried to court her, she would at first respond to the flattery, but then turn on the admirer when they did not follow her instructions or balked at her presumptions. She upbraided, excoriated, and harassed any critics or biographers who nosed unbidden around her literary property.

Marriage to Schuyler Jackson, and the move to Florida, seemed to offer peace to this woman who suffered under a sense of beleaguerment, who caused drama and upset wherever she went. But the 1986 preface to her last book belies the notion that she could escape her demons, even in the Florida wilderness: "I have been caused weighty pain by the Enemy, the indistinct and its false lying shapes of distinctness, as it has sway in the world of intellectual (literary, scholarly) life. The weight of the pain of personal injury has kept dissolving itself in the pain of consciousness of wide-spread falsifications of the human state enveloping it in the lie of its being itself a pandemonium in which peace and pleasure can only be achieved by techniques of treating it as a painfully absurd state—in which peace and pleasure can be no more than contrived stupefactions."[12]

It rather sounds that, by escaping to Florida, Riding Jackson was able to conceal from the world the fact that she had lost her bearings completely in her obsession with falsehoods. But was falsehood, to her, another word for style?

*

In 1942, Auden told Louise Bogan that he considered her, Eliot, Moore, and Laura Riding the four best American poets.[13] In the late 1980s, John Ashbery devoted one of his Charles Eliot Norton lectures to Riding. There is a stubborn residue of the poetic that endures despite her attempts to scrub it from respectability. It is obvious in the Riding poem that Auden is most indebted to—for its meter, rhythm, abstractions, and negations—in such works as "On Sunday Walks…" and "Law Like Love." It is called "All Nothing, Nothing":

> The standing-stillness,
> The from foot-to-foot,
> Is no real illness,
> Is no true fever,
> Is no deep shiver;
> The slow impatience
> Is no sly conscience;
> The covered cough bodes nothing,
> Nor the covered laugh,
> Nor the eye-to-eye shifting
> Of the foot-to-foot lifting,
> Nor the hands under-over,
> Nor the neck and the waist
> Twisting loose and then tight,
> Right, left and right,
> Nor the mind up and down
> The long body column
> With a know-not-why passion
> And a can't-stop motion:
> All nothing, nothing.

Ashbery asks, "What then are we to do with a body of poetry whose author warns us that we have very little chance of understanding it, and who believes that poetry is a lie?" His ready reply: "Why, misread it, of course, if it seems to merit reading, as hers so obviously does."[14]

Yes, he's right. If poetry, as Riding Jackson would have it, is a misreading of the world, then the only riposte is to misread the misreading. It is a concession to her deepest misgivings—that poetry isn't the way to an implacable, objective—one might even say fundamentalist—"truth." And yet what it contains is more than merely "vanities" or "linguistic felicity." Remembering Frost's definition of style—"that which indicates how the writer takes himself and what he is saying"—Riding Jackson's claim that poetry could do no more than approach "the style of truth"[15] seems like an evasion of style's crucial significance: its ability to reveal the writer's soul—her ease or dis-ease *with herself*—to the reader more directly than the content of the words themselves. It was "the one important thing to know," said Frost. She wanted to set the parameters of the reader's interpretations; she wanted to be in control. But it is impossible to have perfect control of another person's perceptions and interpretations, just as it is impossible to be perfectly transparent to oneself.

Perfect mastery, in art, is an illusion. One of poetry's great mysteries is its frequent appeal to outside forces, like Caedmon's and Rilke's angel, or Lorca's Duende, the Muses and the Castilian springs. Greek and Roman epics called out to the gods for inspiration—to be used as a medium or vessel for insight into nature. The act of close reading, putting poets and poems side by side and teasing out the hidden correspondences, is less a scholarly enterprise than a religious one: it assumes that such correspondences are not accidental, but planted there by independent minds who perceived the same things across vast distances of time and space.

This principle underlies the relationships between the poets in this book; they are linked in a personal chain of correspondences: between Stevens and Moore, between Moore and Bishop, between Bishop and Merrill, and, more speculatively, between Merrill and Mathews (time may yet reveal more scholarship on this point, but their interest in formalism links them indelibly). Riding Jackson would seem like a broken link here.

Yet in literary history, there are correspondences that don't have or need personal affection to explain them. Years ago, I was asked by a librarian at Harvard's Woodberry Poetry Room to write something about their online "Vocarium," recordings of poets reading their poetry. I ended up choosing two recordings to compare. They were of Riding Jackson and Merrill.

I acknowledged that Riding Jackson and Merrill are two poets one seldom reads side by side. They were of different generations (born twenty-five years apart), temperaments (she a cerebral Modernist, he an autobiographical aesthete), and upbringings (she the daughter of Austrian Jewish immigrants, he the scion of an American financier from Florida). But there are overlaps. Both were born in New York City and fled to Europe as young adults; both spent significant time in the Mediterranean, steeped in classical mythologies. Both ended up with partners named Jackson!

I couldn't find any evidence that they ever met: by the time Merrill went to college, Riding Jackson was already settled in Wabasso.

Yet, it struck me that there was some point of contact between Laura Riding's thirty-line poem "Doom in Bloom," which according to Robert Graves's diary, was written around September 1937, and Merrill's thirty-one-line poem "The Greenhouse," first published in 1952. Both poems were written in their authors' twenties; they were very young.

"Laura has been having trouble with her poem now called Doom in Bloom & did little else all day but 8 lines of it," wrote

Graves on September 21.[16] When you listen to her read it, you notice the British clip of her voice, acquired somewhere between 1926 and 1939 and still prominent in 1972, the year of the recording. You also notice the precision with which she enunciates and the briskness of the whole performance. The coldness with which she reads is thrilling with respect to this dark spell of a poem, but it suggests, too, a distance from the obvious difficulty of it—the difficulty of its meaning; the difficulty of writing it on that long-ago afternoon in 1937; and the difficulty of inhabiting it now after her momentous change of heart.

"The Greenhouse," in contrast, is much more sensual, and Merrill's languid reading is entirely of a piece with its lush reverie. But it, like "Doom in Bloom," contains much that is obscure—or, better yet, camouflaged.

Both poems hide an allegory about womanhood under elaborate phrasings like tangled vines—"Gruesomely joined in hate/Of unlike efflorescence"; "Down ferned-faint-steaming alleys of lady slipper"—mimicking the floridity of their subject. We guess that these are about sexual maturation. There is a difference, though, in tone—Merrill's is romantic, while Riding's is full of "ultimate misgiving." Both have a fairy tale quality to them: the fronds "touch my arm," Merrill says; it evokes the nursery rhyme: *Mary, how does your garden grow?...pretty maids all in a row.* But his fairy tale takes place in a hothouse. Riding's is all witchery: "Now flower the oldest seeds." They seem to want to stay in the ground; there is a "long reluctance." But "time has knit so hard a crust" that the seeds must "speak and differ" lest they die in the ground "in pride encased."

What really strikes me is the way in which both poems distinguish a "one" from a multitude of sameness. There is a subtler allegory in these poems than the passage from girlhood to womanhood. Flowers are copies of each other. They are a mass of conformity. Merrill begins: "So many girls vague." He repeats, later in the poem: "So many women." They are all beautiful, but all interchangeable. The turning point in the poem comes with his exclamation:

> Tell me (I said)
> Among these thousands which you are!

Who is he speaking to? The *One*, as we say: the soulmate, the bride, "the proud love fastened on." As the poem ends, it predicts that her cohort, all those masses of beautiful, interchangeable others, will be allowed to rot so that "none shall tempt, when she is gone."

And Riding, too, selects one from her masses of conformist florets:

> The lone defiance blossoms failure,
> But risk of all by all beguiles
> Fate's wreckage into similar smiles.

What is her "one" defying? What is the "risk" that the others take? I think it is reproduction. All of them are reluctant to do it, but "hope makes a stronger half to beauty" and the majority choose to propagate their kind despite "peril." Knowing how risky childbirth used to be, it's no wonder that a woman would subliminally fear reproduction. But there is another, existential aspect to this fear—that one's very singularity is put at risk by reproducing. This is the singularity by which we are loved and loved alone—as Merrill's poem elaborates. (As it happens, neither of them became a parent.)

Looking back on this bit of poetic correspondence I teased out between Riding and Merrill, I get a little chill; I want to whistle past the graveyard, as Emily Dickinson might say.

Is this rejection of fertility also a covert rejection of peacock poetry, the poetry of abundance, the poetry, if you will, of Florida?

In Merrill's case, as we have seen, it is quite the opposite. But in "Doom in Bloom" we see the example of the sumptuous vegetable world as a threat to autonomy—and it's not Riding's only evocation of flowers and death. In "The Flowering Urn," she speaks of "fertility's lie" the way she will later speak of poetry's lie. What is this lie? That the life force is triumphant over death; that art redeems the brevity of life. "It speaks of fruits that could not be," she writes of her own "flowering urn," drawing on Keats's image of eternal beauty.

Yet may we say that in Riding Jackson we have a negative body of Floridian poetry? A poetry we can only speculate on in its absence, keeping in mind that one of her favorite rhetorical moves was litotes, the *no* and the *not* in sentence construction that cannot help but evoke what it attempts to suppress?

> No suit and no denial
> Disturb the general proof.
> Logic has logic, they remain
> Locked in each other's arms,
> Or were otherwise insane,
> With all lost and nothing to prove
> That even nothing can live through love.

After all, the others—Stevens, Bishop, Merrill, Mathews—came and went. They weren't regional poets; they escaped to Florida, used it to fecundate their imaginations, and left, returning only to leave again. Riding Jackson stayed. And the regional poetry she didn't write nevertheless gives a negative charge to the shadowy outline of her five decades in Wabasso.

*

Near the end of his life, Schuyler Jackson wrote to his daughter from a previous marriage, Griselda, that he had watched the first space rocket launch in Cape Canaveral from their front lawn.[17]

Behind this meditation on Laura Riding Jackson is a memory I have until now suppressed: a memory of my earliest glimpse of Florida in 1981 with my parents and three siblings. I was eleven years old and it was our first and only trip to Disney World.

I barely remember the theme park, but I can still recall vividly the miles and miles of orange groves we drove through in a rental car. It was the first time I'd ever seen an orange tree. They were human-sized trees, slender and compact, heavy with fruit. It was early January. I was clutching a little stuffed Bambi, which I imagined would have liked to bound away, fleetly, through the orchards.

Where were we going? It wasn't clear to me. It was one of the ways my parents relieved the dire buildup of tension in a squabbling family of six: driving for its own sake, "going on a car ride," for hours. So I was befuddled when we turned into a lush, leafy lane with strange tropical foliage caressing the windows. In front of us was a building bedecked with flags from all over the world. And that's where the memory stops—of a building very like a visitor's center draped with many-colored banners.

When I asked my mother, decades later, where we had gone that day, she solved the mystery: "It was Cape Canaveral. Your father wanted to see the rockets." She reminisced. "We were all bored and starving, but he took his time. He had to see every exhibit."

And it seemed to me then that my memory of an empty, cavernous visitor's center was suddenly populated with rocket ships and space shuttles. Just like that. And I remembered the tedium, my acquiescence, the resignation of a child who has all her life been subject to the whims of adults. I didn't care about the rockets. I couldn't understand the appeal of space, that dark abstraction, when the globe had such greenery even in January—miles of orange groves laden with golden suns. So I, with a budding poet's license, erased them.

I still see it in my mind's eye when I read Stevens's lines: "A hand that bears a thick-leaved fruit,/A pungent bloom against your shade." 1981 at Cape Canaveral: this was the nearest I came to the living Laura Riding Jackson's orbit. And even then, I knew that outer space was not that fabled place "where people really know how to live."

Endnotes

Chapter 1

1. G. R. Stewart, 448
2. H. D., 183
3. Stevens, *Collected Poetry and Prose*, 901
4. O'Hara, *The Collected Poems of Frank O'Hara*, 197
5. O'Hara, *Early Writing*, 116
6. Auden, *Dyer's Hand*, 338
7. Ibid, 71
8. Frost, *Collected Prose, Poems, and Plays*, 702
9. Braden, *Sixteenth Century Poetry: An Annotated Anthology*, 513
10. Brazeau, 160
11. Winters, 262
12. Gunn, 11
13. *The Oxford History of Poetry in English*, 434
14. Spenser, *The Works of Edmund Spenser*
15. Trudeau-Clayton, 26
16. Samuel Johnson's dictionary, 7
17. Daniel, *A Defense of Rhyme*
18. Miller, 4
19. Ibid, 62
20. Merrill, *Collected Prose*, 527
21. Ibid
22. Ibid, 528
23. Braden, 513
24. Martland, 32
25. Dolar, 75

Chapter 2

1. Richardson, 120
2. Brazeau, 224n79
3. Ibid, 62, 81
4. Ibid, 40
5. Ibid, 41
6. Stevens, *Letters*, 233
7. Brazeau, 99
8. Ibid, 99
9. Ibid, 99
10. Ibid, 104
11. Ibid
12. Ibid
13. Ibid, 101–2
14. Rawlings, 106–7

15. Brazeau, 103
16. Stevens, *Letters*, 308
17. Ibid, 191
18. Ibid, 225
19. Stevens, *Collected Poetry & Prose*, 336, 344
20. Stevens, *Letters*, 288–89
21. Ibid, 790
22. Ibid, 306
23. *Oxford Dictionary of English*, 1412
24. Stevens, *Letters*, 449
25. Ibid, 294
26. Ibid, 351–52
27. Ibid, 352
28. Stevens, *Collected Poetry & Prose*, 764
29. Stevens, *Letters*, 247
30. Ibid, 274
31. Ibid, 278
32. Ibid, 449–50
33. Stevens, *Collected Poetry & Prose*, 97
34. Ibid
35. Ibid

Chapter 3

1. Hall
2. *Poetry* magazine: https://www.google.com/books/edition/Poetry/YQ4nAQAAIAAJ?hl=en&gbpv=1&dq=%22This+volume+is+the+study+of+a+Marco+Polo+detained+at+home.%22&pg=PA209&printsec=frontcover
3. Stevens, *Letters*, 279
4. Ibid, 277
5. Stevens, *Collected Poetry & Prose*, 775
6. Moore, *Complete Prose*, 583
7. Wilson, 5
8. Payne, 63
9. Kagan, 66
10. Ibid, 78
11. Ibid, 70–71
12. Ibid, 125
13. Ibid, 59
14. Ibid, 105
15. Ibid, 107
16. Wilson, 6
17. Ibid, 150
18. Ibid, 132
19. Hall, 54
20. Kreymborg, 238-3
21. Wilson, 153–54
22. Ibid, 157
23. Arber, 30
24. Brodsky, 82
25. Ibid, 84
26. Stevens, Letters, 288–89
27. Alexander, 64
28. Ibid, 55

NOTES TO PAGES 65–100   149

29. Bartram, LII
30. Bartram, 104
31. Coleridge, 118
32. Ibid., 25

Chapter 4

1. Bishop, *One Art*, 53
2. Ibid, 57
3. Ibid, 89
4. Ibid, 53
5. Bishop, *Poems, Prose, and Letters*, 729
6. Bishop, *One Art*, 106
7. Ibid, 79
8. Bishop, unpublished journals
9. Ibid
10. Ibid
11. Bishop, *One Art*, 115
12. Bishop, *Poems, Prose, and Letters*, 24–25
13. Bishop, *Journals*
14. Bishop, *One Art*, 151–52
15. See, for instance, Campbell, "Elizabeth Bishop and Race in the Archive"
16. Bishop, *One Art*, 88
17. Fountain and Brazeau, 72
18. Bishop, *One Art*, 549
19. Ibid, 478
20. Stevens, *Letters*, 272
21. Brazeau, 100–101
22. Ibid, 100
23. Bishop, *Journals*
24. Ibid
25. Frost, *Collected Prose, Poems, and Plays*, 702
26. Bishop, *Journals*
27. Ibid
28. Bishop, *One Art*, 71
29. Kalstone, 94
30. Ibid, 81
31. Bishop, *Journals*
32. Bishop, *Poems, Prose, and Letters*, 862
33. Merrill, *A Whole World*, 329
34. Bishop, *Poems, Prose, and Letters*, 852
35. See Campbell, "Elizabeth Bishop and the Literary Archive," 131–50
36. Yenser, 121
37. Bishop, *One Art*, 57

Chapter 5

1. Bishop, *Journals*
2. Merrill, *Collected Prose*, 231
3. Bishop, *Journals*
4. Merrill, *Collected Prose*, 219
5. Merrill, *A Whole World*, 119
6. James, 724
7. Yenser, 39

8. Merrill, *Collected Prose*, 61
9. Hammer, 15–16
10. Yenser, 4
11. Merrill, *The Changing Light at Sandover*, 174
12. Ibid, 6–7
13. Bishop, *Letters*, 23
14. Calasso, 30
15. Ibid, 60
16. S. Stewart, 91–92
17. http://www.wraengineering.com/florida-springs-protection-awareness-month/
18. https://www.nparks.gov.sg/nparksbuzz/issue-19-vol-4-2013/conservation/the-secret-life-of-dragonfly-larvae

Chapter 6

1. Cather, 135
2. Pound, 25
3. "Hymn to Dionysus": https://www.perseus.tufts.edu/hopper/text?doc=Perseus%3Atext%3A1999.01.0138%3Ahymn%3D7%3Acard%3D32
4. Hunnewell, 83
5. Mathews, *The Case of the Persevering Maltese: Collected Essays*, 85
6. Mathews, Collected Poems, xi
7. Introduction to reading: https://media.sas.upenn.edu/pennsound/authors/Mathews/Sienese-Shredder-2006/Mathews-Harry_02_Comatas_Sienese-Shredder_2006.mp3
8. Saint Phalle, 120–22
9. Ibid, 110
10. Ibid, 22
11. Ibid, 125
12. Hunnewell, 85
13. Calasso, 31
14. https://media.sas.upenn.edu/pennsound/authors/Mathews/Sienese-Shredder-2006/Mathews-Harry_02_Comatas_Sienese-Shredder_2006.mp3
15. Hunnewell, 81
16. Ibid, 101
17. Ibid, 94
18. Ibid, 94
19. Merrill, Collected Prose, 210
20. Even with means, it is not easy to maintain aesthetic independence. Bishop had a note appended to the copyright page of North & South when it was published 1946: "Most of these poems were written, or partly written, before 1942." In a letter to her publisher, Houghton Mifflin, in 1945, she explained: "The fact that none of these poems deal directly with the war, at a time when so much war poetry is being published, will, I am afraid, leave me open to reproach. The chief reason is simply that I work very slowly. But I think it would help if a note to the effect that most of the poems had been written before 1941 could be inserted at the beginning, say just after the acknowledgements" (Bishop, Poems, Prose, and Letters, 932).
21. Levy, 17

Chapter 7

1. "Cracker house" is the designated term for the simple wood-frame houses built in Florida by early poor white settlers, despite the racialized, pejorative origins of the word.

2. Baker, 416
3. Ibid, xvii
4. Ibid, 165
5. Ibid, xiii
6. Jackson, Reader, xvi
7. Ibid, 417
8. Riding, *Rational Meaning*, 11
9. Ibid
10. Riding Jackson, *The Failure of Poetry*, 110
11. Ibid, 112
12. Riding, *Rational Meaning*, 12
13. Smith, 48
14. Ashbery, 101–2
15. Riding Jackson, *The Laura Riding Jackson Reader*, xix
16. Graves, The Robert Graves Diary Project, searched by keywords
17. Baker, 419

Bibliography

Caroline Alexander, *The Way to Xanadu: The Search for the Sources of Coleridge's Kubla Khan*, Weidenfeld & Nicholson, 1993
Edward Arber, *Some Longer Elizabethan Poems*, University of Michigan, 1909
John Ashbery, *Other Traditions*, Harvard University Press, 2001
Wystan Hugh Auden, *The Dyer's Hand*, Vintage/Random House, 1989
Deborah Baker, *In Extremis: The Life of Laura Riding*, Grove/Atlantic, 1992
William Bartram, *The Travels of William Bartram*, ed. Francis Harper, University of Georgia Press, 1998
Elizabeth Bishop:
    One Art: Letters, selected and ed. Robert Giroux, Farrar, Straus and Giroux, 1994
    Poems, Prose, and Letters, Library of America, 2008
    Unpublished journals, anticipated publication by Farrar, Straus and Giroux in 2026
Gordon Braden, *Sixteenth Century Poetry: An Annotated Anthology*, Blackwell Publishing, 2005
Peter Brazeau, *Parts of a World: Wallace Stevens Remembered*, Random House, 1983
Joseph Brodsky, *Watermark*, Farrar, Straus and Giroux, 1989
Roberto Calasso, *Literature and the Gods*, Vintage/Random House, 2001
Marvin Campbell, "Elizabeth Bishop and Race in the Archive," in Bethany Hicok (ed.), *Elizabeth Bishop and the Literary Archive*, Lever Press, 2019
Helen Carr, *The Verse Revolutionaries: Ezra Pound, H.D., and the Imagists*, Jonathan Cape, 2009
Willa Cather, *Willa Cather in Europe*, ed. George Norbert Kates, University of Nebraska Press, 1988
Samuel Taylor Coleridge, *A Choice of Coleridge's Verse*, ed. Ted Hughes, Faber & Faber, 1996
Samuel Daniel, *A Defense of Rhyme (1603)*
René de Laudonnière, "L'Histoire notable de la Floride, 1586
Mladen Dolar, *A Voice and Nothing More*, MIT Press, 2006
Gary Fountain and Peter Brazeau, *Elizabeth Bishop: An Oral Biography*, University of Massachusetts Press, 1994
Robert Frost, *Collected Poems, Prose, & Plays*, Library of America, 1995
Thom Gunn, *Shelf Life: Essays, Memoirs, and an Interview*, University of Michigan Press, 1993
Robert Graves, Diary 1935–39, The Robert Graves Diary Project, https://graves.uvic.ca/

Langdon Hammer, *James Merrill: Life and Art*, Knopf, 2015
H.D., *End to Torment: A Memoir of Ezra Pound*, New Directions, 1979
Susannah Hunnewell, "Harry Mathews: The Art of Fiction No. 191," *The Paris Review, Issue 180*, Spring 2007
Laura Riding Jackson:
   The Failure of Poetry, the Promise of Language, University of Michigan Press, 2007
   The Laura (Riding) Jackson Reader, Elizabeth Friedmann (ed.), Persea, 2005
   Rational Meaning: A New Foundation for the Definition of Words, University of Virginia Press, 1997
Henry James, *Collected Travel Writings: Great Britain and America*, Library of America, 2014
Samuel Johnson, *Dictionary of the English Language (1755)*, https://johnsonsdictionaryonline.com/
Ben Jonson, *Poetaster*, Manchester University Press, 1996
Richard L. Kagan, *Lucrecia's Dreams: Politics and Prophecy in Sixteenth-Century Spain*, University of California Press, 1995
David Kalstone, *Becoming a Poet: Elizabeth Bishop, with Marianne Moore and Robert Lowell*, Farrar, Straus and Giroux, 1989
John Keats, *The Complete Poems*, Penguin Classics, 1988
Alfred Kreymborg, *Troubadour: An Autobiography*, Sagamore Press, 1957
Deborah Levy, *The Cost of Living: A Working Autobiography*, Bloomsbury, 2018
Peter Martland, *Since Records Began*, University of California Press, 1997
Harry Mathews:
   Case of the Persevering Maltese: Collected Essays, Dalkey Archive Press, 2003
   Collected Poems: 1946–2016, Sand Paper Press, 2020
James Merrill:
   The Changing Light at Sandover, Knopf, 2006
   Collected Poems, Knopf, 2001
   Collected Prose, Knopf, 2004
   A Different Person, Knopf, 1993
   A Whole World: Letters from James Merrill, Knopf, 2021
Lucasta Miller, *Keats: A Brief Life in Nine Poems*, Knopf, 2022
Marianne Moore:
   Complete Prose, Viking Penguin, 1986
   A Marianne Moore Reader, Viking Penguin, 1961
   Observations, Farrar, Straus and Giroux, 2016
Catherine Nicholson, *Uncommon Tongues: Eloquence and Eccentricity in the English Renaissance*, 2013
Frank O'Hara:
   The Collected Poems of Frank O'Hara, Alfred A. Knopf, 1971
   Early Writing, Grey Fox Press, 1977
Oxford Dictionary of English, 2010
The Oxford History of Poetry in English, eds. Catherine Bates and Patrick Cheney, Oxford University Press, 2022
Edward John Payne, ed., *Voyages of Hawkins, Frobisher and Drake: Select Narratives from the "Principle Navigations" of Hakluyt*, Forgotten Books, 2018

BIBLIOGRAPHY

Ezra Pound, *The Spirit of Romance*, New Directions, 2005
The Princeton Encyclopedia of Poetry and Poetics, 3rd ed., eds. Alex Preminger, Terry V.F Brogan, and J. Warnke, Princeton University Press, 1993
Marjorie Kinnan Rawlings, *Cross Creek Cookery*, Atria Books, 1996
Joan Richardson, *Wallace Stevens: The Later Years*, William Morrow, 1988
Niki de Saint Phalle, *Harry and Me, 1950–1960: The Family Years*, Berteli Verlag, 2006
Stan Smith, ed., *The Cambridge Companion to Auden*, Cambridge University Press, 2005
Edmund Spenser, The Works of Edmund Spenser, Vol. 2, ed. Henry John Todd, 1805

Wallace Stevens:
  Collected Poetry & Prose, Library of America, 1997
  Letters of Wallace Stevens, selected and ed. Holly Stevens, University of California Press, 1966

George R. Stewart, *Names on the Land*, NYRB Classics, 2008
Susan Stewart, *The Ruins Lesson*, University of Chicago Press, 2021
Michel Tournier, *Friday*, Johns Hopkins University Press, 1997
Margaret Tudeau-Clayton, *Shakespeare's Englishes: Against Englishness*, Cambridge University Press, 2019
Derek Walcott, *The Poetry of Derek Walcott 1948–2013*, Farrar, Straus and Giroux, 2014
Thomas Wilson, *The Art of Rhetoric (1560)*, ed. Peter E. Medine, Pennsylvania State University Press, 1994
Violet Wilson, *Queen Elizabeth's Maids of Honour*, John Lane, 1922
Yvor Winters, *The 16th Century Lyric in England: A Critical and Historical Reinterpretation:Part I, Poetry*, Vol. 53, No. 5, (February 1939)
Stephen Yenser, *The Consuming Myth: The Work of James Merrill*, Harvard University Press, 1987

Acknowledgments

I wrote *Difficult Ornaments* largely during the spring and summer of 2021, after a year of pandemic lockdown. Some of the close readings of Merrill, Moore, Mathews, and Riding Jackson were adapted from previous pieces published in *Poetry* and *The London Review of Books*, as well as the Poetry Foundation and the Woodbury Poetry Room Vocarium at Harvard University.

Without the support of Jonathan Galassi, who gave me access to the as-yet-unpublished journals of Elizabeth Bishop, this book would never have come to be. I am supremely grateful for his trust, guidance, and friendship.

Sarah Chalfant, Luke Ingram, and Jacqueline Ko at the Wiley Agency gave me much-needed advice and impetus to finish the manuscript when I was stuck. Without their belief in this project, it would still be a file on my laptop.

My editor at Oxford, Hannah Doyle, proved to be the perfect reader for *Difficult Ornaments*, and I thank her, Brent Matheny, and their team at Oxford.

I am grateful to Arlo Haskell and the Key West Literary Seminar for a residency in the early stages of research, which allowed me to visit Bishop's, Merrill's, and Mathews's houses.

Thanks to David Mikics for reading an early draft. Thank you to Marsha Bryant for moral support and the rest of my colleagues in the English Department at the University of Florida, whose dedication to teaching has been steadfast through much stormy weather.

And thank you to my sons, Jacob and Gray, for their invaluable perspectives, their good humor, their love and affection.

ACKNOWLEDGMENTS

I would like to thank Penguin Random House for permission to reproduce lines from Wallace Stevens's "Esthetique du Mal" and James Merrill's "The Victor Dog," as well as Arlo Haskell and Marie Chaix for permission to reproduce lines from Harry Mathews's "Cool Gales Shall Fan the Glades." I thank also Persea Books for permission to reproduce Laura Riding Jackson's "All Nothing, Nothing" from *The Poems of Laura Riding*.

Index

Since the index has been created to work across multiple formats, indexed terms for which a page range is given (e.g., 52–53, 66–70, etc.) may occasionally appear only on some, but not all of the pages within the range.

aestheticism 48, 76–8, 105. *See also* decadence
Alexander, Caroline 64–5
allegory 38–41, 99–100, 103, 141–2
Allen, Ross 94–5
Allende, Lucas de 55
Andrade, Carlos Drummond de 89–90
animals 47–8, 62–4. *See also* individual animals by name
apostrophe 77–8
artifice 58–9, 83–4, 103–7
Ashbery, John 116–17, 138–9
Auden, W. H. 6, 10–11, 72–3, 136–9
avant-garde 47–8, 111, 116–17

Bach, Johann Sebastian 23–4
Baker, Deborah 134
Barraud, Francis 21–2
Bartram, William 64–6
Baudelaire 84, 91–2
Beardsley, Aubrey 48
beauty 3, 10–11, 27–8, 30, 37, 51, 63, 99–102, 141–2. *See also* ornament; ugliness
Beckett, Samuel 118–19
Bernstein, Leonard 104–5
biology 17, 28, 34–6, 41–2, 47–9. *See also* nature; ornament
Bishop, Elizabeth ix, 19–23, 28, 72–4, 93–5; in Brazil 89–90; in Florida 69–71, 74–82, 84–92; relationship with Moore 69–76, 84–5, 87; relationship with Stevens 69–72, 75–8, 82–3, 87–9; style of 83–91
Bishop, Elizabeth, works by: *An Anthology of Twentieth-Century Brazilian Poetry* 89–90; "The Bight," 77–8, 91–2; *Brazil to Life* 89–90; "Filling Station," 22, 80–1; "The Fish," 84–7, 89; "Florida," 2, 69–72, 76–7; "Jerónimo's House," 80–3; "Key West," 79–80; "Little Exercise," 77–8; "The Man-Moth," 22; *North & South* 89; "One Art," 68, 89; "Roosters," 84–7; "Seascape," 71–2; "Sestina," 80–1; "Songs for a Colored Singer," 80–1; "The Street by the Cemetery," 69
Bloch, Ernest 22–3
Blough, Frani 84
Boccaccio, Giovani 100–2
Boethius 24–5
Bogan, Louise 138–9
Brandeis, Irma 17–18
Brazeau, Peter 31
Brazil 89–90
Brodsky, Joseph 62–3
Browne, Sir Thomas 84

160   INDEX

Burford, William 107
Byron, George Gordon,
    Lord 9–10, 17, 26

Caedmon 61
Calasso, Roberto 107–8, 120–1
Calvino, Italo 117
Carr, Helen 3–4
Catullus 26
Chaix, Marie 128–9
Chaucer, Geoffrey 17
chimeras 62–4, 99, 110. See also
    Moore, Marianne
Church, Henry 42
citation 103–4
climate 7–8; language and 38–43;
    of mind and planet ix
climate change 87–8
close reading 139
Coleridge, Samuel Taylor 16,
    64–7, 95–6
comedy 24–5, 42
Confessional poetry 130
Congreve, William 100–2, 113
cosmopolitanism 89–90
Crane, Hart 135–6
Crane, Louise 68–71, 74
Cuba 89–90

Daniel, Arnaut 112–13
Daniel, Samuel 16
Dante (Alighieri) 12–13, 24–5,
    100–2, 112–13
Dare, Virginia 6–7
Darwin, Charles 63
Davies, Sir John 11–12, 18–19,
    62–3
decadence 13, 48. See also
    aestheticism
Denby, Edwin 116–17
Depression 82, 98–9
description 87–9
Dial, The (magazine) 47

dispossession 73–4, 81–3
Dowland, John 126–8
Drake, Francis 55–6
dread 5–7
dreams 55–6

ekphrasis 119–21
Eliot, T. S. 3, 52, 120–1, 133–4
elitism 117
Elizabeth I, Queen 6–7, 52–4,
    56, 58–62
embroidery 58–9
emotion 28
Empson, William 136
entertainment 22
environment 105–7
evolution 34, 41–2. See also
    ornament
excess 100
exoticism 80–1
experimentation. See play
extinction 87–8

fabliau 34
Florida 5–11; Alachua sink 66–7;
    Cape Canaveral 143–5; Disney
    World 144; Dry Tortugas 1;
    exploration of 64–7; Fountain of
    Youth 97; Gainesville 8, 66–7;
    Garrison Bight 90–2; history
    of 1–2; Kanapaha Plantation
    8–10; Key West ix, 1, 44–6,
    72–83, 85–7, 89–92, 104–5, 111–12,
    124–6, 128–31; Keys 33–4, 44–6,
    111–12, 128–9; Matanzas
    River 7–8, 54–5; Miami 33–4,
    44; mythography of 97–8; Palm
    Beach 95–7, 104; Payne's
    Prairie 66–7; peacocks and 27;
    poetry of ix–x, 2–3, 12–13, 28, 34,
    37, 42–4, 52–4, 64–5, 67, 69–73,
    76–90, 95–107, 111–12, 124–6,
    134–5, 142–5; Silver Springs

94–5, 103; St. Augustine 7–8;
  Sweetwater Overlook 66–7;
  University of Florida 51–2, 134–5
form 28, 37–9, 116–17, 126–8
Fredericks, Claude 17–18
Friendship ix
Frost, Robert 10–13, 84, 139
Fugitive, The (magazine) 135–6

Gascoigne, George 15–16
Gaskell, Arlo 90–1
Geoffrey of Vinsauf 18–19
Geography 38–44, 64–7, 72–3,
  77–80, 87–90, 96–102, 128–9
George, King 65–6
Giacometti, Alberto 118–19
Giroux, Robert 91–2
Graves, Robert 124–6, 133–7,
  140–1
Guest, Barbara 116–17
Gunn, Thom 12–13

Haile, Serena Chesnut 8–10
Haile, Thomas Evans 8–9
Hall, Donald 47–8, 58–9
Hammer, Langdom 102
Handel, George Frideric 109–11,
  113–42
"Have you not hard of floryda?,"
  52–4, 69–71
Hawkins, Sir John 52–5, 64–6
Hawthorne, Nathaniel 55
H.D. (Hilda Doolittle) 3–4, 48–9
Herbert, George 84
Herodotus 58–9
Herrick, Robert 16
HIV/AIDS 99
Hogarth Press 135–6
Homer 115–16
homosexuality 100–2
Hopkins, Gerard Manley 84
Horace 13–15, 18–19
Hughes, Ted 65–6, 113–39

Hunt, Leigh 16
hurricanes 2, 5, 54–5, 77, 81–2

illusionism 60–1
imagination 6, 22, 52–4, 61–4, 88–9
Inquisition 55–6
islands 1, 69, 75–6, 79, 91–2

Jackson, David 102, 104–5
Jackson, Schuyler 132–3, 143
James, Henry 58–9, 95–6
Jarrell, Randall 130
Johnson, Samuel 16
Jonson, Ben 13–15, 38–9, 41–2

Kagan, Richard L. 57
Kalstone, David 85, 87–8
Keats, John 16, 97–8
Koch, Kenneth 116–17

landscape 87–90, 95–7
language: adaptation and 34;
  climate and 38–43; music
  and 126; play and ix–x, 22–5,
  117; poetry and ix–x, 1–2, 9–26,
  28, 34–43, 47, 58–9, 83–5, 100,
  102–4, 114–15, 117, 126, 132–7;
  weather and ix. *See also
  under* poetry
Latimer, Ronald Lane 36–7,
  42–3, 50
Laudonnière, René de 54
León, Lucrecia de 55–8
Levy, Deborah 130–1
Lispector, Clarice 89–90
litotes 143
Lowell, Robert 3, 77–8

manatees 105–7
Marvell, Andrew 115–16
Mathews, Harry ix, 28; in
  Florida 124–6, 128–30; style
  of 116–17, 126–8, 130–1

162 INDEX

Mathews, Harry, works by:
  Cigarettes 116, 128; "Comatas,"
  118–24; *The Conversions* 116;
  "Cool Gales Shall Fan the
  Glades," 110–16, 121–2, 124–6;
  The Journalist 116; "Male
  Chauvinist," 126–8; "Marriage
  of Two Minds: Received
  Visions," 126–8; "The Monkey at
  the Wheel," 126; "Multiple
  Choice," 126–8; *My Life in the
  CIA* 116; "The Pines and Son
  Beltran," 124–6; *The
  Planisphere* 110–11; "The
  Politicians' Antic Spoil," 128;
  "The Relics," 124–6; *The
  Ring* 118; "Selected Declarations
  of Dependence," 126–8; *The
  Sinking of the Odradek
  Stadium* 116; *The Solitary
  Twin* 116; *Tlooth* 116–17; "Trial
  Impressions," 126–8; "Up to
  Date," 126–8
May, Philip 32
McIntosh, David 25–6
Mediterranean 111–12, 124–6,
  128–9
Medusa (magazine) 107–8
Mendoza, Alonso de 55, 57–8
Merrill, James ix, 28, 87–8, 93–5,
  107–8, 128–9, 140; death 98–9; in
  Florida 94–107; style of 102–5
Merrill, James, works by: "Annie
  Hill's Grave," 100–2; "Black
  Swan," 100; "The Broken
  Home," 103; *The Changing Light
  and Sandover* 100–2, 105;
  "Clearing the Title," 104;
  "Developers at Crystal
  River," 105–7; *A Different
  Person* 17–18; *First Poems*
  99–100; "From the Cupola,"
  95–6, 103–4; "The Greenhouse,"
  140–2; "Lost in Translation,"
  95–6, 103–4; "The Parrot," 100;
  "The Peacock," 99–100;
  "Pearl," 19–21; "The Pelican,"
  100; "Quatrains for Pegasus,"
  98–9; "The Thousand and Second
  Night," 100–2; "Transfigured
  Bird," 100; "Two from
  Florida," 100–3; "The Victor
  Dog," 21–6; *Water Street* 100–2
Merrill, Charles 94–5, 99–100, 102
Merrill, Hellen Ingram 94–5, 102
metaphor 16, 18–19, 58–9, 97–100,
  103–4, 112–13
metonymy 18–21, 28, 44–6,
  77–81, 85–7
Metropolitan Museum of Art 59–61
Miller, Lucasta 16
Miller, Margaret 74
mimesis 36–7
Mitchell, Joan 118–19
Modernism 2–3, 48, 52, 133–4
Monroe, Harriet 44, 48–50
Montale, Eugenio 17–18
Moore, Marianne ix, 3–4, 28, 47–9,
  60, 69–76, 80–1, 84–5, 87; in
  Florida 47, 64; relationship with
  Stevens 48–51
Moore, Marianne, works by: "The
  Accented Syllable," 48;
  Observations 47–8, 63; "On
  Wallace Stevens," 51; *Poems*
  48–9; "Sea Unicorns and
  Land Unicorns," 47–8, 51–4,
  58–9, 61–5; "The Steeple-Jack,"
  51; "To the Peacock of
  France," 48
morality 63
Morse, Samuel French 44–6
Mueller, Wilhelm 23
Mysticism 93–4

Nashe, Thomas 16
Nast, Condé 102
natural history 69–71

nature: artifice and 103–4; form and 37–8; ornament and ix–x, 17, 27–8, 34–7, 41–3, 47; poetry and ix–x, 17, 28, 34, 37–8, 41–3, 47, 63–4, 85–7, 103–4, 132–3. *See also* ornament; poetry
New Criticism 3, 136
New York school 116–17
Norton, Charles Eliot 138–9
nymphs 107–8, 120–1

O'Dowd, Charles 30
O'Hara, Frank 5, 116–17
order 77
ornament ix–x, 17, 27–8, 34–7, 39, 41–3, 52, 58–9, 87–8; difficult 18–22, 25–6, 28, 100, 112–13
Others (journal) 48
Oulipo 116–17
Ouvroir de littérature potentielle 117
Ovid 113–42

palm trees 2, 27, 29, 33–4, 44–6, 68–72, 76–8, 95–7, 129
Paris Review 47–8
Parrhasius 60–1
pastoral 110
Paz, Octavio 89–90
peacocks ix–x, 26–7, 29, 34–6, 47–8, 51, 77, 84–7, 99–102, 105–7. *See also* animals
Perec, Georges 113, 117
Philadelphia (Pennsylvania) 3–5
Philip II, King 55–6
place ix, 3–13
plantations 8–10
Plath, Sylvia 3
play ix–x, 22–5, 37–9, 117
poetry 97–8; form and 37–9, 116–17, 126–8; geography and ix, 3–5, 38–44, 64–7, 72–3, 77–80, 87–90, 96–102, 128–9; language

and ix–x, 1–2, 9–26, 28, 34–43, 47, 58–9, 83–5, 100, 102–4, 114–15, 117, 126, 132–7; meter 22–3, 86–7, 138–9; nature and ix–x, 17, 28, 34–8, 41–3, 47, 63–4, 85–7, 103–4, 132–3; observation and 87–9; ornament and ix–x, 17–22, 25–6, 28, 34–7, 39, 41–3, 47, 58–9, 100, 112–13; peacocks and 26–7; play and 117; rhyme 28, 37–8, 58–9, 84–7, 93–4; truth and 113, 133–4, 139. *See also under* Florida; language; nature
Poetry (magazine) 48–9, 110–11
Ponce de León, Juan 1, 97
Pope, Alexander 25, 110, 113
Porter, Anne and Fairfield 116–17
Pound, Ezra 3–4, 17, 112–13, 115–16, 120–1
Powell, Arthur 30–2, 82–3
primitivism 89–90
privacy 74–5, 93
prophecy 97–8
puns 18–21, 23–4, 105–7
Pythagoras 24–5

Queneau, Raymond 117, 126–8

race 80–3
Raine, Kathleen 133–4
Raleigh, Sir Walter 6–7, 9–10, 63
Ransom, John Crowe 135–6
Rawlings, Marjorie Kinnan 5–6, 32
Reagan, Ronald 105
reality, realism 36–7, 39–41, 52–4, 72–3, 76–8, 80–4, 87–9, 103–4
regionalism 82–3
reproduction 34, 142
reveille 86–7
Riding Jackson, Laura ix, 132–3, 135–7, 139–40; in Florida 132–5, 137–8, 143–5; renunciation of poetry 132–4

Riding Jackson, Laura, works by: "All Nothing, Nothing," 138–9; *A Close Chaplet* 135–6; *Contemporaries and Snobs* 133–4; "Doom in Bloom," 140–3; "The Flowering Urn," 142–3; "The Promise of Words," 136–7; *Rational Meaning* 134–5; *A Survey of Modernist Poetry* 136; "World's End," 143
Rilke, Rainer Maria 103–4
Rimbaud, Arthur 134
Riopelle, Jean-Paul 118–19
Roanoke Island 6–7
romanticism 52, 72–3, 87–90
Rosenbach Museum 60
Roussel, Raymond 116–17

Sainte Phalle, Niki de 116, 118–19, 121–2, 124–6
Schubert, Franz 23
Schumann, Robert 23–4
Schuyler, James 116–17, 137
Seaver, Bob 74, 91–2
sestina 111–13, 116, 128
settlements 5–8
sexism 117
Shakespeare, William 16, 43–4; *The Tempest* 39, 75–6, 91–2
Shelley, Percy 17
Sidney, Sir Philip 26, 90–1, 128
simile 28, 113–14
Simons, Hy 42–3
slavery 8–10, 52–4
sonnet 11–12, 126–8
Spanish–American War 43–4
Spenser, Edmund 15–16
Spillane, Mickey 47
springs 97–9, 108
stanza 19–21, 28, 80–1, 93–4, 100, 111–13

Stein, Gertrude 3
Stevens, Wallace ix, 3–4, 16, 28–9, 48, 64, 69–73, 75–8, 87–9, 93–5, 100, 134; in Florida 30–4, 44–6, 82–3; relationship with Moore 48–51
Stevens, Wallace, works by: "Anecdote of the Prince of Peacocks," 34–6; "The Bird with the Coppery, Keen Claws," 34–8; "Cattle Kings of Florida," 43–4; "The Comedian as the Letter C," 38–43, 52–4; "The Countryman," 4; "Disillusionment of Ten O'Clock," 124–6; "Fabliau of Florida," 34, "A Farewell to Florida," 44–6; "A Fish-Scale Sunrise," 34, 77–8; "From the Journal of Crispin," 31–2; *Harmonium* 34–9, 49–50, 69–71, 76–7, 124–6; "Hibiscus on the Sleeping Shores," 49–50; "Homunculus et la Belle Etoile," 37–9, 76–7; "The Idea of Order at Key West," 34, 37–8, 82–3; *Ideas of Order* 44–6; "Indian River," 34; "Like Decoratiosn in a Nigger Cemetery," 82–3; "Mozart [1935]," 31–2; "Nomad Exquisite," 2, 34, 71–2; "Notes Toward a Supreme Fiction," 34, 124–6; "O, Florida, Venereal Soil," 34; "A Poet That Matters," 51; "Two Figures in Dense Violet Night," 71–2
Stevenson, Anne 87, 89
Stewart, George R. 1–2
Stewart, Susan 108
Stuart, Mary 56
Sturges, Preston 31

style ix, 10–17, 25–6, 28, 57, 83–5,
  87–8, 90–1, 102; ethics of 80–3,
  88–9; peacock 26–7, 34–7
Sutherland, Donald 90–1
Swenson, May 81–2
Symonds, J. A. 58–9

Tate, Allen 135–6
Theocritus 124
Tinguely, Jean 118
tourism 44
Tournier, Michel 6
trompe l'oeil 60–1
tropics ix–x, 12–13, 34–6, 39–42,
  71–2, 79–80
troubadours 12–13, 112–13, 116
truth 113, 133–4, 139

ugliness 77–8, 80–1. See also beauty
unicorns 47–8, 52–4, 58–9, 61–3

Valéry, Paul 95–7, 103–4
Venus 34, 37–8, 64

Wagner, Richard 126
Walcott, Derek 7–8
Wanning, Thomas Edwards 77–8
weather ix, 38–9, 132. See also
  climate
White, John 6–7
Williams, William Carlos 3, 133–4
Wilson, Thomas 15–16
Wilson, Violet 51–5, 58–9, 61–3
Winters, Yvor 12–13, 48–9
work 22–3
Wyatt, Thomas 17

Yeats, William Butler 3
Yenser, Stephen 100, 102–3

Zeuxis 60–1